I0009145

ExcelAutomateReport©

Automatically prepare reports with just a few clicks !!!

By Ceyvian C

Website : www.eOfficeSolutionz.com

Email : careline@eofficesolutionz.com

ISBN-10: 1463583869

ISBN-13: 978-1463583866

First Published : June 2010

Version : 1.1

Level : Intermediate Level

Applies to : Microsoft Excel 2000, 2003 & 2007

Written with:

This book is written with Excel 2003. However, the formulas & concept work in Excel 2000 & 2007 too.

The only dissimilarity is on where the buttons & functions located in Excel 2007 as Excel 2007 has changed its interface.

About the Author

My name is Ceyvian. I am the author of ***ExcelAutomateReport*** and owner of **eOfficeSolutionz.com**. I was major in Marketing and have been working in different companies from different industry & environment. As a marketing personnel, I did a lot of analysis & performance tracking for the product and marketing programs I handled to evaluate the result achieved.

In my first job, I worked as a Product Executive cum Purchaser in a distributor company that carries IT products from well-known brands. I handled 5 major brands and we were required to meet the quota set by our Principal/Vendor. I had to generate & tabulate a lot of reports in order to analyze or measure the performance of the brands I was assigned to. It was very tedious & hectic as I had to overlook the product performance, running marketing programs, tabulate the marketing programs milestone & result, initiate purchase & forecasting, evaluate dealer performance and etc for each brand. Therefore, I started to find ways to reduce the time to get these important data analyzed & yet generate the report in the layout or format that best suit my needs, management requirements or even company objectives. I was successful by getting the report to automate itself.

Then I moved on to one of the IT Principal Company as Business Partner Manager. My main role was to handle trade marketing programs for the appointed distributors. I had to do a lot of reports in a wide angle in this position. Besides evaluating the trade marketing programs' effectiveness & performance, I need to measure their individual target for each product line and business unit, take into consideration their inventory level state, do ranking and etc to ensure that the trade marketing programs that were rolled out is sufficient in assisting the distributors to 3rd tier dealers in achieving their target set. The situation get complex here because I was facing difficulties in the different ways of obtaining the data in this company. Some data is obtained from Reporting Tool, some is obtained from the customers by sending files over and some is obtained from another department of the company. I continued striving to get all these reports generated without required much time and of course the best is to automate them. Finally I was successful again after much exploration by combining the formulas in the application.

After sometime, I moved to my third job in a Principal Company as well but this is a non-IT Principal Company. They don't even have a system to capture & store information. All information is tracked by data key-in into spreadsheet or in hardcopy documents. However it was not a problem for me this time, because I know how to handle and place the data I need in my spreadsheet with the ***ExcelAutomateReport*** concept that I have created.

From there onwards, whichever company I joined later on, I am able to adapt my ***ExcelAutomateReport*** concept in my work regardless of the nature of business / company. I just sit back & relax while waiting my report to be generated automatically. Nevertheless, I feel so good, productive and efficient at all times.

Contents

1.0 Introduction

This chapter will give you a preview on what is *ExcelAutomateReport* about.

Example 1
A purchaser need to find out the company's stock status and propose to the boss the quantity to order with a supporting document before proceed to raise a purchase order.

Then the purchaser downloads the relevant data from the company system into an excel file sheet as follow:

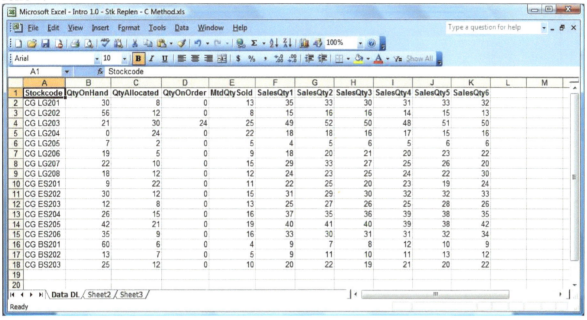

Next, the purchaser open the vendor price list file and match back the pricing for each stockcode either by VLOOKUP or manually key-in next to the data downloaded, evaluate the stock status, propose the order and lastly insert formula calculation in the same sheet. This process will be repeated every time when the purchaser wants to check stock status.

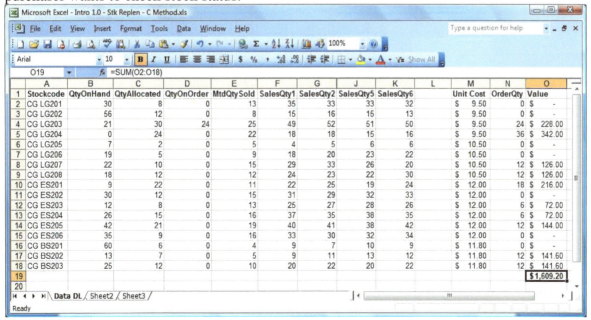

With **ExcelAutomateReport** method, the purchaser can download the data in an excel sheet.

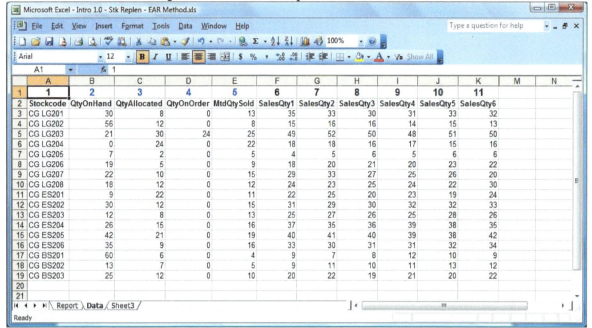

And get the report automatically generated every time in another sheet by doing a template and insert combined formula using ExcelAutomateReport method for the first time only.

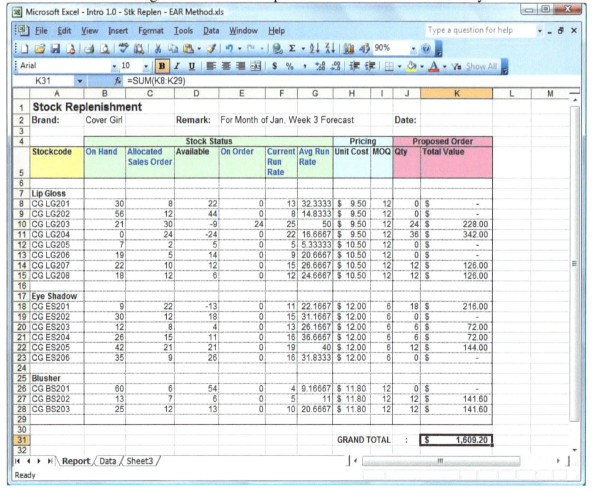

Example 2

A Product Manager / Sales Manager needs to find out up-to-date program performance / sales team performance weekly where individual target is set for each sales person.

The manager downloads the relevant up-to-date data from the company system into an excel file sheet as follow:

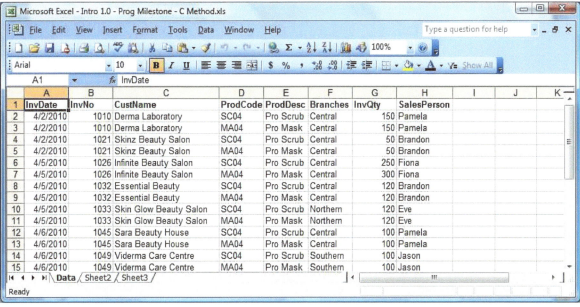

Then the manager tabulates the data using pivot table (laid out in Column A-D) and analyze the program / sales team performance by inserting formula in Column F & G. The manager needs to repeat this process every week when updating the latest data.

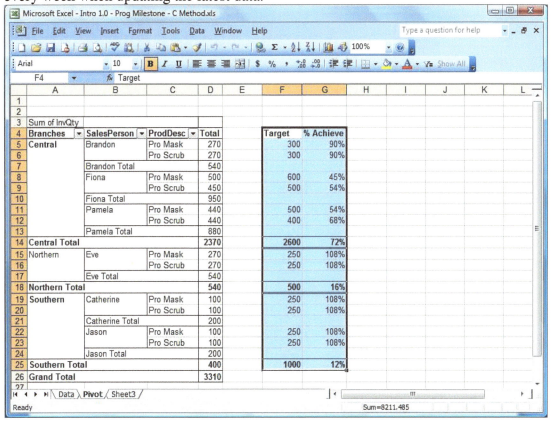

With **ExcelAutomateReport** method, the manager can download the data in an excel sheet.

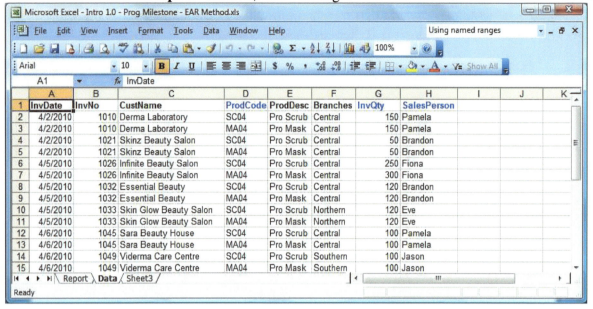

And get the report automatically generated every time in another sheet by doing a template and insert combined formula using ExcelAutomateReport method for the first time only.

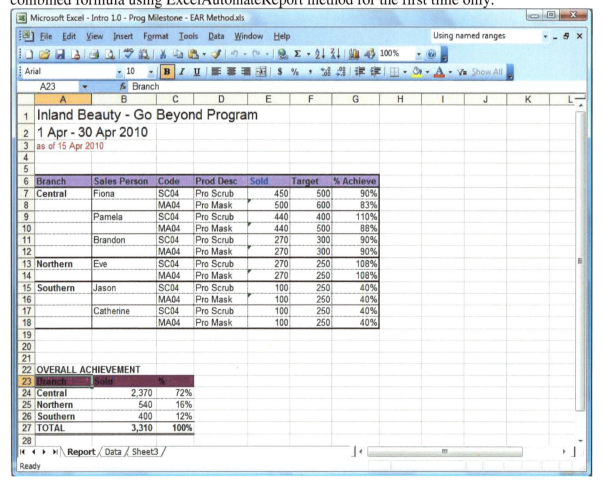

Example 3

A marketing personnel want to find out the different kind of number of participants in a program.

The marketing personnel sort the list and count the number of participants manually.

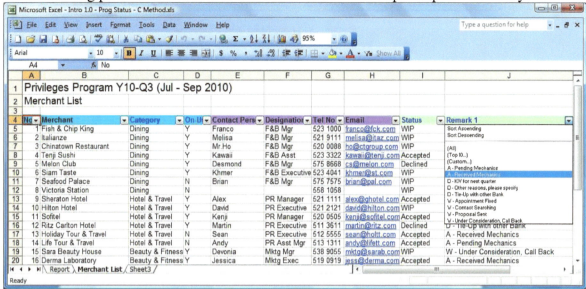

And then, enter the counted number to the summary report one by one until finish counting the different kind of participants.

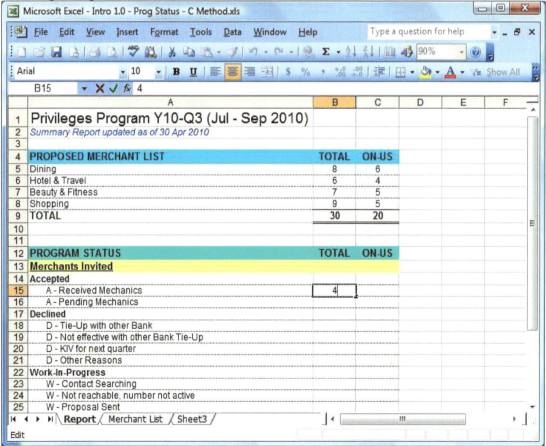

With **ExcelAutomateReport** method, the number of participants will be counted automatically in the report sheet from the list as and when the list is being updated.

Again, this can be done by doing a report template and insert combined formula using **ExcelAutomateReport** method for the first time only.

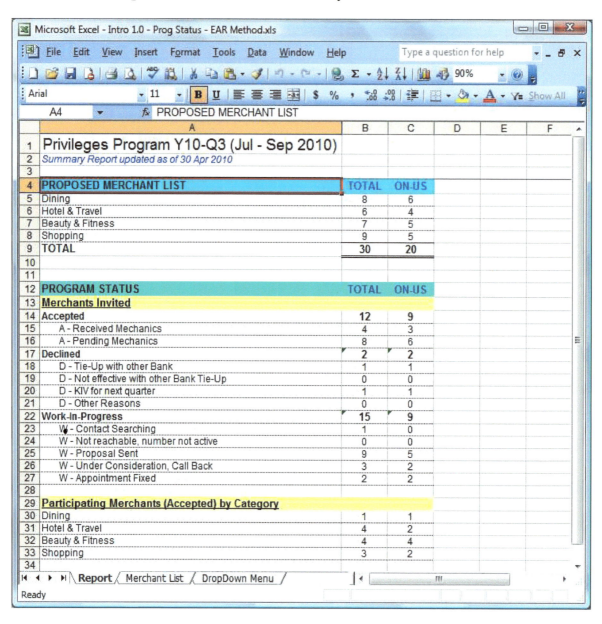

Benefit of ExcelAutomateReport

In conclusion, using ExcelAutomateReport can benefit you in many ways:
1. Time Saving, Efficiency & Increase Productivity
2. Meet Management Requirements / Company Objectives
3. Better Presentation
4. Self Preferences layout instead of Excel Pre-Set layout

1. Time Saving, Efficiency & Increase Productivity

Compare to the conventional/usual method, ExcelAutomateReport help you save hours of time to prepare either daily, weekly, bi-weekly, monthly or even ad-hoc reports.

You just need to do the report template once. After that, just sit back and relax, the report will be automatically generated for you once the updated data is finished downloaded / imported.

Nevertheless, you don't have to go through the pain and boringness of repeating the process again and again to achieve the same report that you wanted to do.

You can always complete the report on time and always project yourself as an efficient employee to the management. With the extra time you have, you can enhance & develop skills in other area in the company to upgrade yourself.

2. Meet Management Requirements / Company Objectives

Most of the times, management will require you to do the report in the format that they require or to align with the company objectives.

Meet Management Requirements

For example, an employee use pivot table to do a report as shown below.
Unfortunately, the Pivot Table format cannot meet management requirements.

	A	B	C	D	E	F	G	H
1								
2								
3				CustName				
4	Category	ProdCode	Data	Inland Beauty	Wooland	Zaza	Grand Total	
5	Cleanser	CL01	Sum of InvValue	56070	21360	21360	98790	
6			Sum of InvQty	630	240	240	1110	
7		CL02	Sum of InvValue	26700	16910	15130	58740	
8			Sum of InvQty	300	190	170	660	
9		CL03	Sum of InvValue	26700	29370	21360	77430	
10			Sum of InvQty	300	330	240	870	
11	Cleanser Sum of InvValue			109470	67640	57850	234960	
12	Cleanser Sum of InvQty			1230	760	650	2640	
13	Mask	MA04	Sum of InvValue	133650	94050	32670	260370	
14			Sum of InvQty	1350	950	330	2630	
15	Mask Sum of InvValue			133650	94050	32670	260370	
16	Mask Sum of InvQty			1350	950	330	2630	
17	Moisturiser	MO01	Sum of InvValue	58050	28380	19350	105780	
18			Sum of InvQty	450	220	150	820	
19		MO02	Sum of InvValue	60630	33540	19350	113520	
20			Sum of InvQty	470	260	150	880	
21		MO03	Sum of InvValue	54180	33540	20640	108360	
22			Sum of InvQty	420	260	160	840	
23	Moisturiser Sum of InvValue			172860	95460	59340	327660	
24	Moisturiser Sum of InvQty			1340	740	460	2540	
25	Scrub	SC04	Sum of InvValue	75650	48950	24920	149520	
26			Sum of InvQty	850	550	280	1680	

Pivot Table can display up to 2 fields only

Invoice Quantity & Value is displayed stacking (vertical) instead of side by side (horizontal)

Note: The field name is fixed too, which is the same with the database field name, cannot be changed.

Management requires the report to show all: product category, product code, product description follow by unit cost for the product portion AND unit & revenue side by side for the sales portion.

It is very time consuming & tedious for the employee to shift the data downloaded to the format required by management manually. Even using VLOOKUP formula, the purchaser need to repeat the VLOOKUP formula steps for many times.

ExcelAutomateReport can help you to automatically retrieve the data from the data downloaded in the report format you want or required by the management.

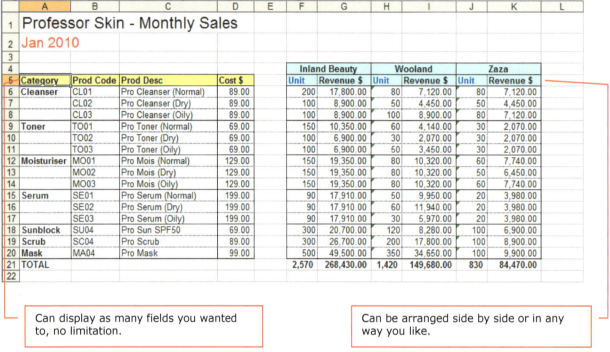

Category	Prod Code	Prod Desc	Cost $		Inland Beauty		Wooland		Zaza	
					Unit	Revenue $	Unit	Revenue $	Unit	Revenue $
Cleanser	CL01	Pro Cleanser (Normal)	89.00		200	17,800.00	80	7,120.00	80	7,120.00
	CL02	Pro Cleanser (Dry)	89.00		100	8,900.00	50	4,450.00	50	4,450.00
	CL03	Pro Cleanser (Oily)	89.00		100	8,900.00	100	8,900.00	80	7,120.00
Toner	TO01	Pro Toner (Normal)	69.00		150	10,350.00	60	4,140.00	30	2,070.00
	TO02	Pro Toner (Dry)	69.00		100	6,900.00	30	2,070.00	30	2,070.00
	TO03	Pro Toner (Oily)	69.00		100	6,900.00	50	3,450.00	30	2,070.00
Moisturiser	MO01	Pro Mois (Normal)	129.00		150	19,350.00	80	10,320.00	60	7,740.00
	MO02	Pro Mois (Dry)	129.00		150	19,350.00	80	10,320.00	50	6,450.00
	MO03	Pro Mois (Oily)	129.00		150	19,350.00	80	10,320.00	60	7,740.00
Serum	SE01	Pro Serum (Normal)	199.00		90	17,910.00	50	9,950.00	20	3,980.00
	SE02	Pro Serum (Dry)	199.00		90	17,910.00	60	11,940.00	20	3,980.00
	SE03	Pro Serum (Oily)	199.00		90	17,910.00	30	5,970.00	20	3,980.00
Sunblock	SU04	Pro Sun SPF50	69.00		300	20,700.00	120	8,280.00	100	6,900.00
Scrub	SC04	Pro Scrub	89.00		300	26,700.00	200	17,800.00	100	8,900.00
Mask	MA04	Pro Mask	99.00		500	49,500.00	350	34,650.00	100	9,900.00
TOTAL					2,570	268,430.00	1,420	149,680.00	830	84,470.00

Professor Skin - Monthly Sales

Jan 2010

> Can display as many fields you wanted to, no limitation.

> Can be arranged side by side or in any way you like.

Besides that, the field name can be changed to the name you preferred too.

Meet Company Objectives

And there are times our reports need to meet company objectives as well. For instance after finish tabulating the data, we need to insert additional information and calculation to check the sales tabulated whether meet the company target OR evaluate the stock inventory and proposed order against company budget / vendor quota and etc.

Like in Example 2 earlier, the product/sales manager need to insert the target set for each sales person and calculate the achievement everytime after the manager tabulate the data using pivot table. This is because sales target (company objectives) is not a fix attribute / field in a database and is a separate set of data set by company, which cannot be downloaded from system to be tabulated together using Pivot Table.

	A	B	C	D	E	F	G	H	I
1									
2									
3	Sum of InvQty								
4	Branches	SalesPerson	ProdDesc	Total		Target	% Achieve		
5	Central	Brandon	Pro Mask	270		300	90%		
6			Pro Scrub	270		300	90%		
7		Brandon Total		540					
8		Fiona	Pro Mask	500		600	45%		
9			Pro Scrub	450		500	54%		
10		Fiona Total		950					
11		Pamela	Pro Mask	440		500	54%		
12			Pro Scrub	440		400	68%		
13		Pamela Total		880					
14	Central Total			2370		2600	72%		
15	Northern	Eve	Pro Mask	270		250	108%		
16			Pro Scrub	270		250	108%		
17		Eve Total		540					
18	Northern Total			540		500	16%		
19	Southern	Catherine	Pro Mask	100		250	108%		
20			Pro Scrub	100		250	108%		
21		Catherine Total		200					
22		Jason	Pro Mask	100		250	108%		
23			Pro Scrub	100		250	108%		
24		Jason Total		200					
25	Southern Total			400		1000	12%		
26	Grand Total			3310					
27									
28									

Normally a company built-in system will not include target, whether it is sales target or vendor quota. Target/Quota is a very subjective issue, impromptu, can be measured in different angles (by SKU/ ProductLine/ Brand/ SalesPerson/ Program) and change from time to time.

As such, ExcelAutomateReport come in handy to help you gathered these separate data together and generate the report automatically for you.

	A	B	C	D	E	F	G	H	I
1	Inland Beauty - Go Beyond Program								
2	1 Apr - 30 Apr 2010								
3	as of 15 Apr 2010								
4									
5									
6	Branch	Sales Person	Code	Prod Desc	Sold	Target	% Achieve		
7	Central	Fiona	SC04	Pro Scrub	450	500	90%		
8			MA04	Pro Mask	500	600	83%		
9		Pamela	SC04	Pro Scrub	440	400	110%		
10			MA04	Pro Mask	440	500	88%		
11		Brandon	SC04	Pro Scrub	270	300	90%		
12			MA04	Pro Mask	270	300	90%		
13	Northern	Eve	SC04	Pro Scrub	270	250	108%		
14			MA04	Pro Mask	270	250	108%		
15	Southern	Jason	SC04	Pro Scrub	100	250	40%		
16			MA04	Pro Mask	100	250	40%		
17		Catherine	SC04	Pro Scrub	100	250	40%		
18			MA04	Pro Mask	100	250	40%		
19									
20									
21									
22	OVERALL ACHIEVEMENT								
23	Branch	Sold	%						
24	Central	2,370	72%						
25	Northern	540	16%						
26	Southern	400	12%						
27	TOTAL	3,310	100%						
28									

3. Better Presentation

ExcelAutomateReport also help you prepare reports in better presentation. Unlike report prepared from data downloaded in a list or using Pivot Table, ExcelAutomateReport let you group items into category, and use of color, border & font formatting to enhance the report appearance will be lasting in the report until you make next changes.

Report prepared from Data downloaded in a list

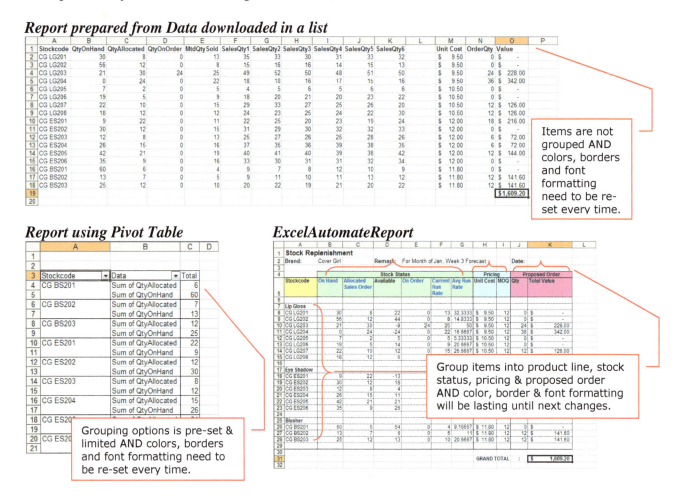

Items are not grouped AND colors, borders and font formatting need to be re-set every time.

Report using Pivot Table

Grouping options is pre-set & limited AND colors, borders and font formatting need to be re-set every time.

ExcelAutomateReport

Group items into product line, stock status, pricing & proposed order AND color, border & font formatting will be lasting until next changes.

4. Self Preferences layout instead of Excel Pre-Set layout

Instead of Excel Pre-Set layout, you have choice to choose your self-preferences layout like arrange the item sequence in the order that you want.

Excel Pivot Table   *ExcelAutomateReport*

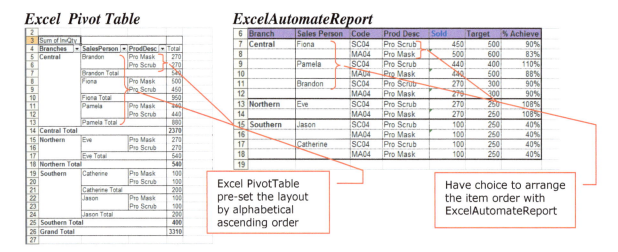

Excel PivotTable pre-set the layout by alphabetical ascending order

Have choice to arrange the item order with ExcelAutomateReport

2.0 Automate Report Concept

ExcelAutomateReport is using **Report** and **Data** separation concept. Meaning, there are 2 parts in ExcelAutomateReport, **Report part** and **Data part** whereby *report* and *data* is separated in an individual sheet in the excel workbook and it is connected to each other. The *report* is a template created with formulas defined by user to retrieve the *data* stored in another separate sheet.

And ExcelAutomateReport always applies the following steps:
Step 1 – Create Report Template
Step 2 – Retrieve Data
Step 3 – Insert Formula
Step 4 – Copy Formula
Step 5 – Evaluation
Step 6 – Save Automate Report

In this chapter, I will give you an overview of the **Report part** which consists of *Report Template* & *Big 5 formulas*. **Data part** will be covered in the next chapter - Chapter 3.

2.1 Report template

ExcelAutomateReport method requires you to create a report template for the first time only. Just create the report in the format and layout you wish and insert the combined formula which the fundamental will be covered in next session under *Big 5 formulas*.

Thereafter, you can sit back and cross your hand to wait for the report to generate automatically for the next update.

2.2 Big 5 formulas

ExcelAutomateReport only use 5 major formulas in the *Report template*, which I term them as *Big 5 formulas*.

This ExcelAutomateReport book is for intermediate level, who has the knowledge of VLOOKUP and also some Excel fundamental formulas. However, I still provide some simple example of the Big 5 formulas on next pages for those beginners to understand the basic if you have never apply such formula before.

The simple example provided often can be found by most of the excel books sold in the market. Normally after understanding the fundamental from the simple example, you find that it is hard or do not know how to apply in your real life working environment.

In this ExcelAutomateReport book, I will cover the real business environment examples beside the simple examples in Chapter 4 – Scenario, where you can apply excel formula successfully in your working environment scenario.

To help you understand better in the simple example provided next, open the workbook 'Fundamental.xls' to try apply the *Big 5 formulas* yourself while going through the simple examples.

1. VLOOKUP

VLOOKUP is use to search for a value in the first column of a table array and returns a value in the same row from another column in the table array. The V in VLOOKUP stands for vertical and is used when comparison values are located in a column to the left of the data that you want to find.

VLOOKUP(lookup_value, table_array, col_index_num, range_lookup)

Arguments	Description
lookup_value	The value to search in the first column of the table array.
table_array	Two or more column of data (search range). The values in the first column of table_array are the values searched by look_up value.
col_index_num	The column number in table_array from which the matching value must be returned. A col_index_num of 1 refer to first column in table_array; a col_index_num of 2 refer to the second column in table_array and so on.
range_lookup	A logical value that specifies whether you want VLOOKUP to find an exact match or an approximate match. To find an exact match, use FALSE so that it will return error value #N/A if no match found, else use TRUE and it will return an approximate match.

Example

To find the order quantity for product code SC04 in Cell H2.

	A	B	C	D	E	F	G	H	I
1	Prod Code	Prod Desc	Cust Name	PO No	PO Qty		Prod Code	PO Qty	
2	CL01	Pro Cleanser	Inland Beauty	10235	200		SC04		
3	TO02	Pro Toner	Inland Beauty	10235	100				
4	MO03	Pro Mois	Inland Beauty	10235	150				
5	SC04	Pro Scrub	Inland Beauty	10235	300				
6	MA04	Pro Mask	Inland Beauty	10235	500				
7									

Type the following VLOOKUP formula in Cell H2.

	A	B	C	D	E	F	G	H	I	J	K
1	Prod Code	Prod Desc	Cust Name	PO No	PO Qty		Prod Code	PO Qty			
2	CL01	Pro Cleanser	Inland Beauty	10235	200		SC04	=VLOOKUP(G2, A2:E6, 5, FALSE)			
3	TO02	Pro Toner	Inland Beauty	10235	100						
4	MO03	Pro Mois	Inland Beauty	10235	150						
5	SC04	Pro Scrub	Inland Beauty	10235	300						
6	MA04	Pro Mask	Inland Beauty	10235	500						
7											

The VLOOKUP formula in Cell H2 finds value "SC04" in first column of table array (A2:E6) and returns the corresponding value in the same row from column 5, which is 300 when the search value match.

H2	▼	*fx*	=VLOOKUP(G2, A1:E6, 5, FALSE)

	A	B	C	D	E	F	G	H	I
1	Prod Code	Prod Desc	Cust Name	PO No	PO Qty		Prod Code	PO Qty	
2	CL01	Pro Cleanser	Inland Beauty	10235	200		SC04	300	
3	TO02	Pro Toner	Inland Beauty	10235	100				
4	MO03	Pro Mois	Inland Beauty	10235	150				
5	SC04	Pro Scrub	Inland Beauty	10235	300				
6	MA04	Pro Mask	Inland Beauty	10235	500				
7									

2. SUM & IF

SUM & IF is use to add numbers based on multiple conditions.

SUM(IF((condition_1)*(condition_2), sum_range))

Arguments	Description
condition_1	First condition to be evaluated to perform the SUM.
condition_2	Second condition to be evaluated to perform the SUM.
sum_range	Add the values in this range provided that the row satisfies the condition 1 & 2.

VLOOKUP can only retrieve data based on 1 condition. When there are 2 conditions or more, we need to use SUM & IF formula.

<u>Example</u>

To find the order quantity for product code CL01 from customer Inland Beauty only.

If use VLOOKUP, it will return the first occurrence "CL01" match which is 200.

	H2		f_x =VLOOKUP(G2, A2:E11, 5, FALSE)						
	A	B	C	D	E	F	G	H	I
1	Prod Code	Prod Desc	Cust Name	PO No	PO Qty		Prod Code	PO Qty	
2	CL01	Pro Cleanser	Inland Beauty	10235	200		CL01	200	
3	TO02	Pro Toner	Inland Beauty	10235	100				
4	MO03	Pro Mois	Inland Beauty	10235	150				
5	SC04	Pro Scrub	Inland Beauty	10235	300				
6	MA04	Pro Mask	Inland Beauty	10235	500				
7	CL01	Pro Cleanser	Inland Beauty	10400	180				
8	MO03	Pro Mois	Inland Beauty	10400	120				
9	CL01	Pro Cleanser	Zaza	10369	80				
10	TO02	Pro Toner	Zaza	10369	30				
11	MO03	Pro Mois	Zaza	10369	60				
12									

If use SUM & IF formula as shown below, it will add up values in E2:E11 which the rows match value "CL01" in A2:A11 and value "Inland Beauty" in C2:C11.

	SUM		=SUM(IF((A2:A11=G3)*(C2:C11="Inland Beauty"),E2:E11))										
	A	B	C	D	E	F	G	H	I	J	K	L	M
1	Prod Code	Prod Desc	Cust Name	PO No	PO Qty		Prod Code	PO Qty					
2	CL01	Pro Cleanser	Inland Beauty	10235	200		CL01	200					
3	TO02	Pro Toner	Inland Beauty	10235	100		CL01	=SUM(IF((A2:A11=G3)*(C2:C11="Inland Beauty"),E2:E11))					
4	MO03	Pro Mois	Inland Beauty	10235	150								
5	SC04	Pro Scrub	Inland Beauty	10235	300								
6	MA04	Pro Mask	Inland Beauty	10235	500								
7	CL01	Pro Cleanser	Inland Beauty	10400	180								
8	MO03	Pro Mois	Inland Beauty	10400	120								
9	CL01	Pro Cleanser	Zaza	10369	80								
10	TO02	Pro Toner	Zaza	10369	30								
11	MO03	Pro Mois	Zaza	10369	60								
12													

Note: The SUM & IF formulas must be entered as array formulas else error #VALUE! or 0 is returned. Press **F2** on keyboard, and then press **CTRL+SHIFT+ENTER**.

Array formulas are enclosed in braces { }. The added value 380 is returned.

	H3		f_x {=SUM(IF((A2:A11=G3)*(C2:C11="Inland Beauty"),E2:E11))}						
	A	B	C	D	E	F	G	H	I
1	Prod Code	Prod Desc	Cust Name	PO No	PO Qty		Prod Code	PO Qty	
2	CL01	Pro Cleanser	Inland Beauty	10235	200		CL01	200	
3	TO02	Pro Toner	Inland Beauty	10235	100		CL01	380	
4	MO03	Pro Mois	Inland Beauty	10235	150				
5	SC04	Pro Scrub	Inland Beauty	10235	300				
6	MA04	Pro Mask	Inland Beauty	10235	500				
7	CL01	Pro Cleanser	Inland Beauty	10400	180				
8	MO03	Pro Mois	Inland Beauty	10400	120				
9	CL01	Pro Cleanser	Zaza	10369	80				
10	TO02	Pro Toner	Zaza	10369	30				
11	MO03	Pro Mois	Zaza	10369	60				
12									

3. COUNTIF / COUNT & IF

COUNTIF is use to count the occurrence of a value in a range of cells, while COUNT & IF is use to count the occurrence of more than once condition.

COUNTIF(range, criteria)

Arguments	Description
range	is the range of cells from which you want to count cells.
criteria	is the condition in the form of a number, expression, cell reference, or text that defines which cells will be counted.

COUNT(IF((condition_1)*(condition_2), blank))

Arguments	Description
condition_1	First condition to be evaluated to perform the COUNT.
condition_2	Second condition to be evaluated to perform the COUNT.
blank	Leave blank for COUNT & IF but must specify the comma [,] before the blank.

Example

Use COUNTIF to count the number of merchants under Hotel & Dining category.

C14		fx	=COUNTIF(C2:C12, "Hotel & Travel")	
	A	**B**	**C**	**D**	**E**
1	No	Merchant	Category	Region	
2	1	Fish & Chip King	Dining	South	
3	2	Chinatown Restaurant	Dining	West	
4	3	Sofitel	Hotel & Travel	East	
5	4	Ritz Carlton Hotel	Hotel & Travel	South	
6	5	Holiday Tour & Travel	Hotel & Travel	East	
7	6	Life Tour & Travel	Hotel & Travel	West	
8	7	Sara Beauty House	Beauty & Fitness	East	
9	8	Derma Laboratory	Beauty & Fitness	East	
10	9	Authentic Spa	Beauty & Fitness	West	
11	10	Rain Hair Studio	Beauty & Fitness	West	
12	11	Fitness Champion	Beauty & Fitness	South	
13					
14		Hotel & Travel	4		
15					

Use COUNT & IF to count the number of merchants under Hotel & Dining category AND in East Region.

C15		fx	{=COUNT(IF((C2:C12="Hotel & Travel")*(D2:D12="East"),))}		
	A	**B**	**C**	**D**	**E**	**F**
1	No	Merchant	Category	Region		
2	1	Fish & Chip King	Dining	South		
3	2	Chinatown Restaurant	Dining	West		
4	3	Sofitel	Hotel & Travel	East		
5	4	Ritz Carlton Hotel	Hotel & Travel	South		
6	5	Holiday Tour & Travel	Hotel & Travel	East		
7	6	Life Tour & Travel	Hotel & Travel	West		
8	7	Sara Beauty House	Beauty & Fitness	East		
9	8	Derma Laboratory	Beauty & Fitness	East		
10	9	Authentic Spa	Beauty & Fitness	West		
11	10	Rain Hair Studio	Beauty & Fitness	West		
12	11	Fitness Champion	Beauty & Fitness	South		
13						
14		Hotel & Travel	4			
15		Hotel & Travel in East	2			
16						

Note: The COUNT & IF formulas must be entered as array formulas else error #VALUE! or 0 is returned. Press **F2** on keyboard, and then press **CTRL+SHIFT+ENTER**. Array formulas are enclosed in braces { }.

4. ISERROR

ISERROR is use to hide the error value.

IF(ISERROR(value, value_if_true, value_if_false))

Arguments	Description
value	refers to any error value (#N/A, #VALUE!, #REF!, #DIV/0!, #NUM!, #NAME?, or #NULL!).
value_if_true	If the formula return error value, show value_if_true .
value_if_false	Otherwise, show value_if_false.

Example

VLOOKUP is used in cell H2 - H6 to find the order quantity for all products. VLOOKUP only found 2 records which is CL01 & TO02 and returned the order quantity in column 5 of A2:E6 table_array. Even order quantity is empty in cell E3 for product code TO02, as long as there is record for the lookup_value, VLOOKUP will return any value in the corresponding column_index_number.

	H3	▼	*fx*	=VLOOKUP(G3, A2:E6, 5, FALSE)					
	A	B	C	D	E	F	G	H	I
1	Prod Code	Prod Desc	Cust Name	PO No	PO Qty		Prod Code	PO Qty	
2	CL01	Pro Cleanser	Inland Beauty	10235	200		CL01	200	
3	TO02	Pro Toner	Inland Beauty	10235			TO02	0	
4							MO03	#N/A	
5							SC04	#N/A	
6							MA04	#N/A	
7							TOTAL	#N/A	
8									

For unfound records, VLOOKUP will returned error value #N/A. Error value #N/A may result in disruption especially when we want to total up all the values. To hide the error value, use ISERROR as follow:

	I4	▼	*fx*	=IF(ISERROR(VLOOKUP(G4, A2:E6, 5, FALSE)), 0, VLOOKUP(G4, A2:E6, 5, FALSE))					
	A	B	C	D	E	F	G	H	I	J
1	Prod Code	Prod Desc	Cust Name	PO No	PO Qty		Prod Code	PO Qty	
2	CL01	Pro Cleanser	Inland Beauty	10235	200		CL01	200	200
3	TO02	Pro Toner	Inland Beauty	10235			TO02	0	0
4							MO03	#N/A	0
5							SC04	#N/A	0
6							MA04	#N/A	0
7							TOTAL	#N/A	200
8									

Note:

ISERROR is practical in VLOOKUP but not in SUM & IF, as SUM & IF will return 0 by default if there isn't any record found to be sum.

5. DEFINE NAME

Define Name is use to refer to a cell or range of cells.

Example
To define name > Select cells range from C2 to D4 > Click Insert > Name > Define.

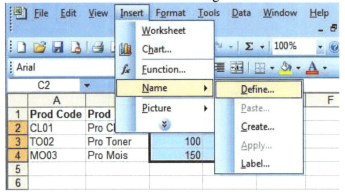

'Define Name' window appeared.
Type 'Order' on the 'Names in workbook' textbox > Click OK.

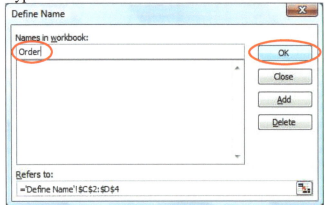

The 'Refers to:' text box by default already have value '='Define Name'!$C$2:$D$4', which means the name 'Order' is referring to cell C2 to D4 in 'Define Name' sheet.

To confirm you have defined name correctly, select cells from C2 to D4 again and check the name box next to formula bar. If it show 'Order', means you have successfully define a name for the range of cells else re-do the step above.

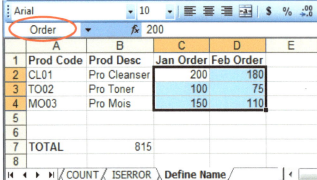

Instead of using 'C2:D4', we can use the defined name 'Order' in the formula.

	B7 ▼	fx	=SUM(C2:D4)	
	A	B	C	D	E
1	Prod Code	Prod Desc	Jan Order	Feb Order	
2	CL01	Pro Cleanser	200	180	
3	TO02	Pro Toner	100	75	
4	MO03	Pro Mois	150	110	
5					
6					
7	TOTAL	815			
8					

It will return the same result.

	B8 ▼	fx	=SUM(Order)	
	A	B	C	D	E
1	Prod Code	Prod Desc	Jan Order	Feb Order	
2	CL01	Pro Cleanser	200	180	
3	TO02	Pro Toner	100	75	
4	MO03	Pro Mois	150	110	
5					
6					
7	TOTAL	815			
8		815			
9					

Important Note:

For *Big 5 formulas* No. 1 – 4, please take note of the " " usage in the formula. Else the formula will not work correctly.

	Required " "	Example (refer example below)
Cell Reference	No	G3
Value in Numeric	No	10235
Value in Non-Numeric (anything other than numeric)		
▪ Text	Yes	"Inland Beauty"
▪ Alphanumeric	Yes	"TO02"

	SUM ▼	=SUM(IF((A2:A11=G3)*(C2:C11="Inland Beauty"),E2:E11))										
	A	B	C	D	E	F	G	H	I	J	K	L	M
1	Prod Code	Prod Desc	Cust Name	PO No	PO Qty		Prod Code	PO Qty					
2	CL01	Pro Cleanser	Inland Beauty	10235	200		CL01	200					
3	TO02	Pro Toner	Inland Beauty	10235	100		CL01	=SUM(IF((A2:A11=G3)*(C2:C11="Inland Beauty"),E2:E11))					
4	MO03	Pro Mois	Inland Beauty	10235	150								
5	SC04	Pro Scrub	Inland Beauty	10235	300								
6	MA04	Pro Mask	Inland Beauty	10235	500								
7	CL01	Pro Cleanser	Inland Beauty	10400	180								
8	MO03	Pro Mois	Inland Beauty	10400	120								
9	CL01	Pro Cleanser	Zaza	10369	80								
10	TO02	Pro Toner	Zaza	10369	30								
11	MO03	Pro Mois	Zaza	10369	60								
12													

3.0 Data

Every individual company stores their data in different ways. No matter how your company stores the data, you can use ExcelAutomateReport method to automate the report for you.

This chapter will give you an understanding of data and how to pull these data out for reporting.

3.1 Raw Data

What is Raw Data?
Raw Data is data which has not been processed and stores in columns and row by row.

Columns are representing fields (or attributes) and Rows are representing records as shown below. And in Database Concept, this is how the data being stores in tables.

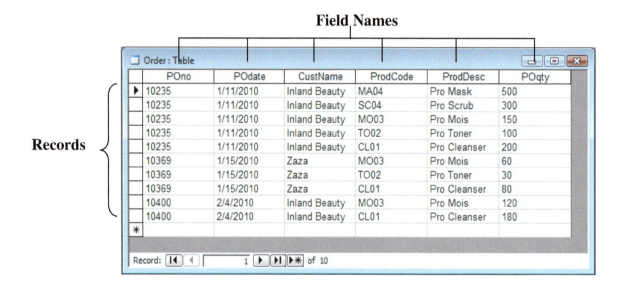

3.2 How to place your Data

We do not have a choice on the company data storage method. This is up to your company on how they store their data and the best way to leverage on this data is to pull it as a raw data instead of pulling the processed data which you pre-tabulate it using some functions of reporting tool.

In this way, you can generate the same report without perform multiple steps everytime you update the report by using ExcelAutomateReport method or use the data to generate different reports later on.

No matter what type of data, just pull the data as raw data in columns and rows into excel file. Excel can contain up to 65,535 rows.

For certain reporting tool that pre-defined the report format already, you might have to delete certain 'Header' rows & 'Footer' rows after you export it to Excel to achieve the raw data format.

Raw Data format / Database format
In order to generate report automatically by using ExcelAutomateReport concept, place your data in raw data format or like database format in Excel.

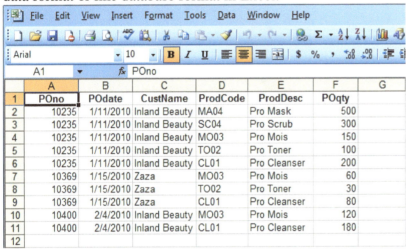

Pre-tabulate format
Don't place data in pre-tabulate format in Excel like the following:

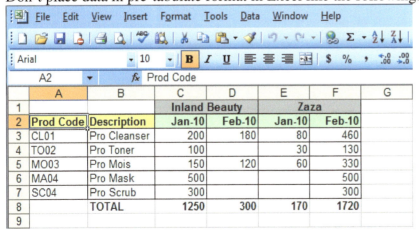

3.3 Type of Data

Lets' go through the different ways the data being stored by different companies and how to place your data in raw format / database format into Excel.

You have probably been briefed on your company data storage method and how to pull them out for reporting usage when you first join your company. If you don't, check with your system administrator so that you know your company belong to which data type below.

3.31 Data import from External Source

Some companies provide connection tool like ODBC driver, OLE DB provider and etc for their employee to import/download them out from database (SQL Server, Oracle, Access and etc) directly into excel spreadsheet for usage.

This is an excellent way because you can choose any fields in the tables from the database and the data will be placed exactly in raw data format / database format in Excel after data import completed.

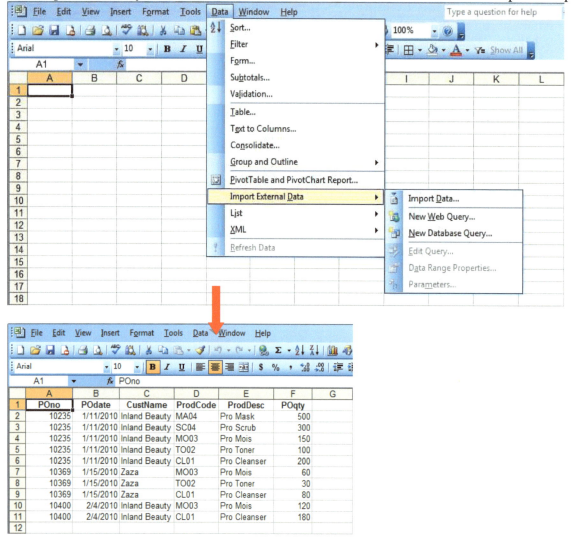

Automate Report with 'Data import from External Source' is covered in Chapter 4, Scenario 1, 2, 3 & 5.

3.32 Data from Reporting Tool

While some companies provide Reporting Tool like Crystal Report, Business Object and etc for their employees to view the data and export the data out. The data can usually be exported in different file format (excel, pdf, rich text format and etc).

The data exported out from Reporting Tool is usually in pre-defined report format with some summary tabulation like the following:

	A	B	C	D	E	F	G
1	Order Report						
2	Date Range : 01-Jan-2010 to 12-Feb-2010						
3							
4							
5	PO Number	PO Date	Customer	Prod Code	Prod Desc	PO Qty	
6	10235	1/11/2010	Inland Beauty	MA04	Pro Mask	500	
7	10235	1/11/2010	Inland Beauty	SC04	Pro Scrub	300	
8	10235	1/11/2010	Inland Beauty	MO03	Pro Mois	150	
9	10235	1/11/2010	Inland Beauty	TO02	Pro Toner	100	
10	10235	1/11/2010	Inland Beauty	CL01	Pro Cleanser	200	
11	10369	1/15/2010	Zaza	MO03	Pro Mois	60	
12	10369	1/15/2010	Zaza	TO02	Pro Toner	30	
13	10369	1/15/2010	Zaza	CL01	Pro Cleanser	80	
14	10400	2/4/2010	Inland Beauty	MO03	Pro Mois	120	
15	10400	2/4/2010	Inland Beauty	CL01	Pro Cleanser	180	
16	Total					1,720	
17							

Delete the 'Header' rows & 'Footer' rows to achieve the raw data format.
'Header' rows – Any rows before the Field row.
'Footer' rows – Any rows after the last records of the data.

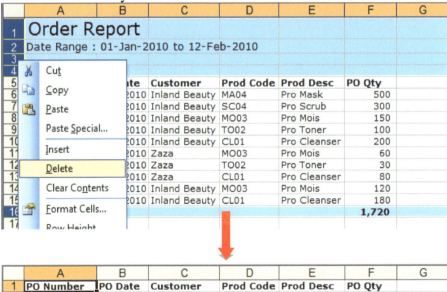

	A	B	C	D	E	F	G
1	PO Number	PO Date	Customer	Prod Code	Prod Desc	PO Qty	
2	10235	1/11/2010	Inland Beauty	MA04	Pro Mask	500	
3	10235	1/11/2010	Inland Beauty	SC04	Pro Scrub	300	
4	10235	1/11/2010	Inland Beauty	MO03	Pro Mois	150	
5	10235	1/11/2010	Inland Beauty	TO02	Pro Toner	100	
6	10235	1/11/2010	Inland Beauty	CL01	Pro Cleanser	200	
7	10369	1/15/2010	Zaza	MO03	Pro Mois	60	
8	10369	1/15/2010	Zaza	TO02	Pro Toner	30	
9	10369	1/15/2010	Zaza	CL01	Pro Cleanser	80	
10	10400	2/4/2010	Inland Beauty	MO03	Pro Mois	120	
11	10400	2/4/2010	Inland Beauty	CL01	Pro Cleanser	180	
12							

Automate Report with 'Data from Reporting Tool' is covered in Chapter 4, Scenario 1, 2, 3 & 5.

3.33 Data in Spreadsheet

However, there are companies that do not have any system & data storage infrastructure at all. The data are key-in by data entry clerk into spreadsheet from paper documents.

In this case, enter the data in database format. Do not key-in the data in the report format you define yourself.

Key-in data in raw data format/database format, row by row into excel spreadsheet.

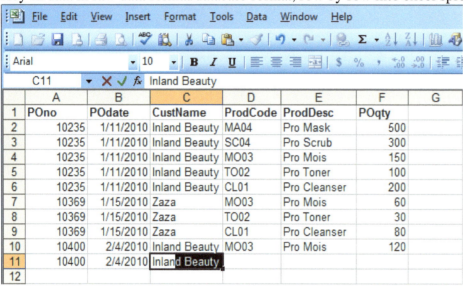

Do not key-in data in the excel spreadsheet where you have defined the report format.

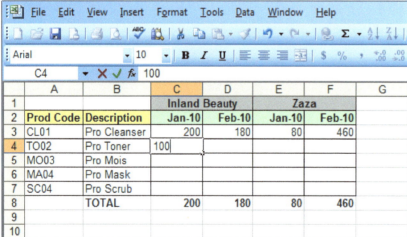

Automate Report with 'Data in Spreadsheet' is covered in Chapter 4, Scenario 4 & 6.

4.0 Scenario

In this chapter, you will see a step-to-step guide on how to do the Automate Report based on my real life working scenario.

As explained earlier in Chapter 2 – Data, each company has their own unique database structure. The field available and the field name are different.

Therefore, you are advised to practice my scenario as tutorial first before you adapt it to your own scenario. Once you understand the concept, then you can apply the Automate Report concept with your scenario by changing it to your company data fields.

In this book, there are 6 scenarios as tutorial for you to master the Excel Automate Report skills. Try all of them step by step to understand the concept. Once you successfully complete the scenario, then try adapting your company's scenario to create the Automate Report.

To make your learning experience more enjoyable & quicker, the excel workbooks / report template for each scenario is available for download and it is absolutely free. Please download the workbook zip file 'Workbook-ExcelAutomateReport.zip' at www.eofficesolutionz.com/order.

You may use the template provided to save your typing time during the tutorial.

Scenario	Workbook
Scenario 1	Stock Replenishment 1.0.xls
Scenario 2	Sales Performance 2.0.xls
Scenario 3	Sales Forecast 3.0.xls
Scenario 4	Product Performance 4.0.xls
Scenario 5	Program Milestone 5.0.xls
Scenario 6	Program Status 6.0.xls

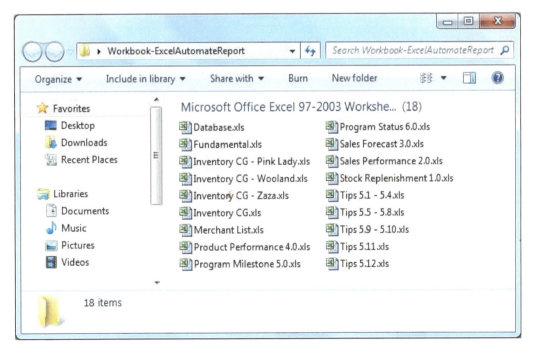

4.1 Scenario 1 : Stock Replenishment Report

Scenario Description
A purchaser in a company requires to find out Stock Status including Inventory, Sales Trend/Run Rate etc to evaluate stock replenishment for a product brand.

Step 1 – Create Report Template

1.1 Open a new excel file & create the report template in Sheet1 OR
   Open the workbook 'Stock Replenishment 1.0.xls' to continue the tutorial.

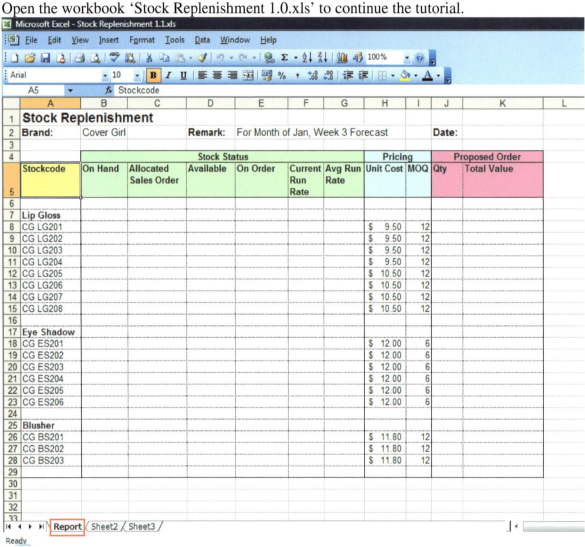

Column A
Stockcode for the Item or the Brand.

Column B, C, E, F, G
These are the columns to retrieve data from the *Raw Data / Database*.

Column D
Column D 'Available' = On Hand – Allocated Sales Order.

If your company branches/sales people can order/book stocks from system, your system will show you 'Allocated Sales Order', where this will be useful to evaluate your stock replenishment by checking the 'On Hand' & 'Allocated Sales Order' to get 'Available'.

Data Field is subject to your company database. Your company database might not have the field 'Allocated Sales Order' or it is under different name.

Column H, I
Other Product Information, like Vendor/Supplier pricing & order MOQ.

Column J, K
These are the column for your decision making later at the last part.

1.2 Rename Sheet1 as 'Report'.

Step 2 – Retrieve Data

2.1 Go to Sheet2 and place your cursor at cell A1 to begin import data.

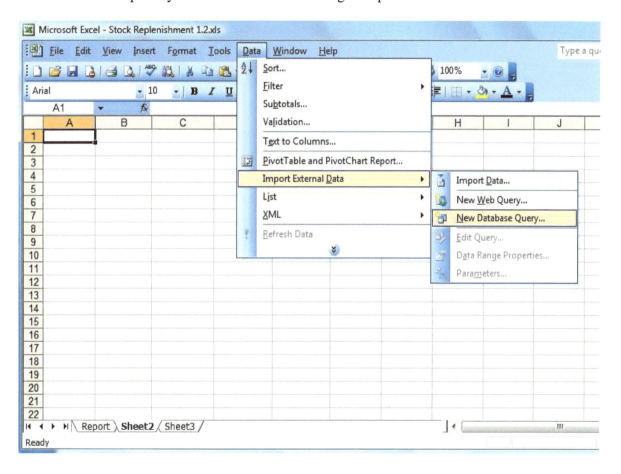

Importing data begin …

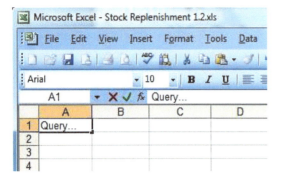

Retrieving data from which source is depending on your company data storage method. Select the relevant tables & fields to import the data.

You may filter the Stockcode criteria if you want to import selected brand only. For example, for Cover Girl brand the stockcode start with CG, then filter Stockcode begins with *CG when you selecting the field. Again, this is depending on how your company creates the stockcode.

If your company data is obtained by reporting tool or in spreadsheet, then just copy & paste the required data in database format as explained earlier in Chapter 3 - Data.

2.2 Rename Sheet2 as 'Data' when data import completed.

For tutorial & learning purpose, the workbook 'Stock Replenishment 1.0.xls' already contained the below data to simulate the data import completed.

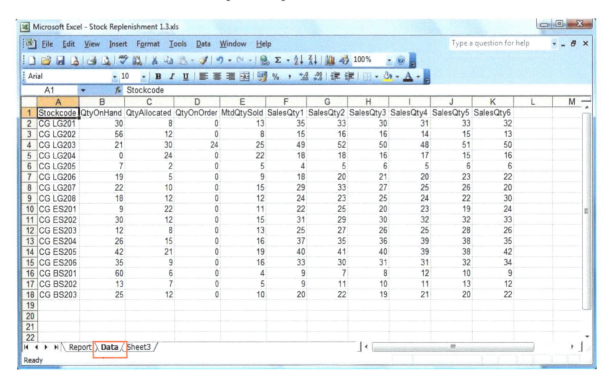

	Stockcode	QtyOnHand	QtyAllocated	QtyOnOrder	MtdQtySold	SalesQty1	SalesQty2	SalesQty3	SalesQty4	SalesQty5	SalesQty6
2	CG LG201	30	8	0	13	35	33	30	31	33	32
3	CG LG202	56	12	0	8	15	16	16	14	15	13
4	CG LG203	21	30	24	25	49	52	50	48	51	50
5	CG LG204	0	24	0	22	18	18	16	17	15	16
6	CG LG205	7	2	0	5	4	5	6	5	6	6
7	CG LG206	19	5	0	9	18	20	21	20	23	22
8	CG LG207	22	10	0	15	29	33	27	25	26	20
9	CG LG208	18	12	0	12	24	23	25	24	22	30
10	CG ES201	9	22	0	11	22	25	20	23	19	24
11	CG ES202	30	12	0	15	31	29	30	32	32	33
12	CG ES203	12	8	0	13	25	27	26	25	28	26
13	CG ES204	26	15	0	16	37	35	36	39	38	35
14	CG ES205	42	21	0	19	40	41	40	39	38	42
15	CG ES206	35	9	0	16	33	30	31	31	32	34
16	CG BS201	60	6	0	4	9	7	8	12	10	9
17	CG BS202	13	7	0	5	9	11	10	11	13	12
18	CG BS203	25	12	0	10	20	22	19	21	20	22

Step 3 – Insert Formula

3.1 Now, the interesting part comes.
Insert a new row at Row 1 in 'Data' sheet and Numbering the columns.

Columns B, C, D, E in 'Data' sheet are the data to be retrieved. Change their font color to Blue to ease you later when inserting formula.

'Data' sheet

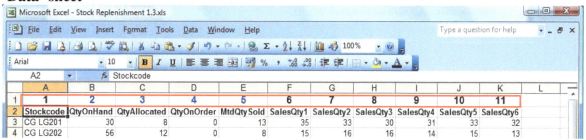

3.2 Go to 'Report' sheet.
Columns B, C, E, F in 'Report' sheet are the column to retrieve the data from 'Data' sheet. Change the font color to Blue as well for easy reference.

'Report' sheet

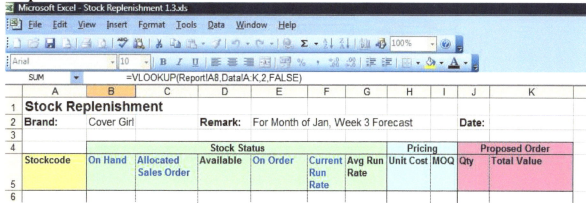

See below table for a better view.

'Report' sheet	Retrieve from	'Data' sheet
[Columns in 'Report' sheet are the columns to retrieve the data from 'Data' sheet. And you can name them what you like.]		[Columns in 'Data' sheet are the columns where the data is imported from a source and to be retrieved to 'Report' sheet. And the columns name appears as what it was named in the database field.]
Column B – On Hand	=	Column B – QtyOnHand
Column C – Allocated Sales Order	=	Column C – QtyAllocated
Column E – On Order	=	Column D – QtyOnOrder
Column F – Current Run Rate	=	Column E – MtdQtySold

Table 4.11

3.3 Insert VLOOKUP formula.

3.31 Click on cell B8. Type in as follow:
=VLOOKUP(A8, Data!A:K, 2, FALSE)

Arguments	Description
A8	The item that you want to search.
Data!A:K	Where your data is placed. The VLOOKUP will search the 'Data' sheet from Column A to K for a match to the item in A8.
2	Which column's value to return from 'Data' sheet when VLOOKUP find a match. The 'On Hand' is in Column No. 2 in 'Data' sheet.
FALSE	To find an exact match only. So that you know if an error message #N/A is displayed, there isn't such records from the data you imported.

Table 4.12

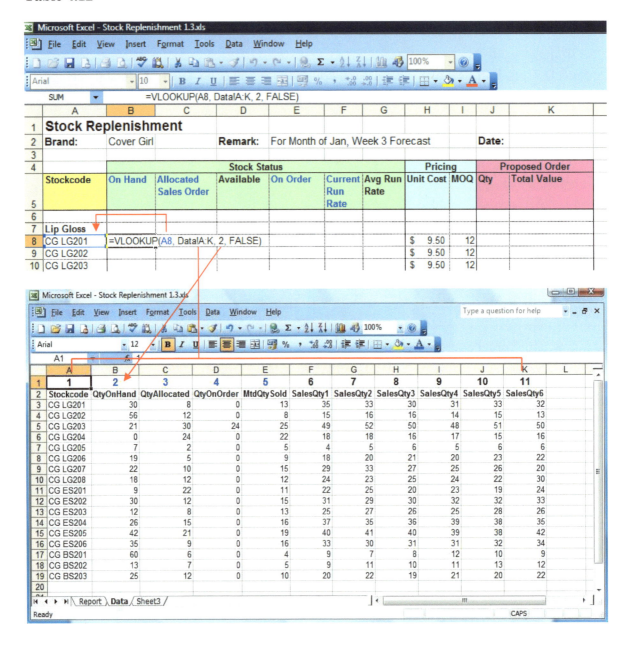

3.32 When the formula complete, press **ENTER** on the keyboard.
The data is successfully retrieved and shown in cell B8.

Note: If error value #N/A is displayed, it means there isn't CG LG201 in the data you imported. You can try by deleting the row that contain CG LG201 (row 3) in 'Data' sheet. To get rid of the error value #N/A, combine VLOOKUP & ISERROR formula which taught in Chapter 2 under 2.2 - *Big 5 formulas*.

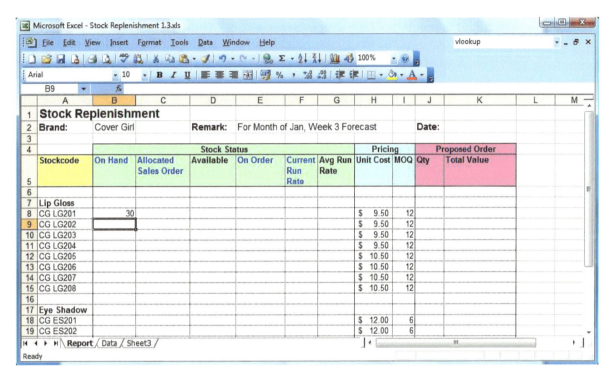

3.33 Repeat Step 3.31 – 3.32 on cell C8, E8 & F8 with the following VLOOKUP arguments:

Cell	Formula
C8	=VLOOKUP(A8, Data!A:K, 3, FALSE)
E8	=VLOOKUP(A8, Data!A:K, 4, FALSE)
F8	=VLOOKUP(A8, Data!A:K, 5, FALSE)

The difference of the formula argument is the Column Number (font highlight in blue above) used to retrieve the data from 'Data' sheet as explain earlier in Table 4.12

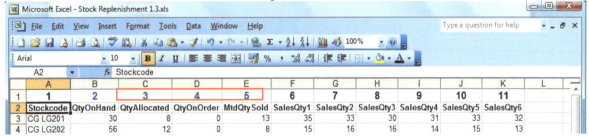

3.4 Insert Other Formula for the remaining columns.

3.41

Column	Description
D	Formula: =B8-C8 As the 'Allocated Sales Order' data is available in my past company, it is useful to deduct the 'Allocated Sales Order' from 'On Hand' stocks to gauge the 'Available' stocks as the allocated stocks are reserved and will be deliver & bill very soon.

Table 4.13

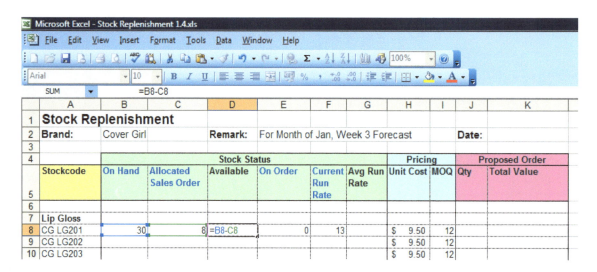

3.42

Column	Description
G	In my past company, the database will store the current month sales & past 6 month sales history: **MtdQtySold** – is month to date qty sold **SalesQty1** – is the last 1 month sales **SalesQty2** – is the past 2 months sales and so on … If these data available, it is useful to get an average sales per month using the past 6 months by insert a formula in Column L in 'Data' sheet. Then insert the VLOOKUP formula in Column G in 'Report' sheet. Formula: =VLOOKUP(A8, Data!A:L, 12, FALSE)

Insert formula in Column L in 'Data' sheet, and number it as 12 and change to blue font.

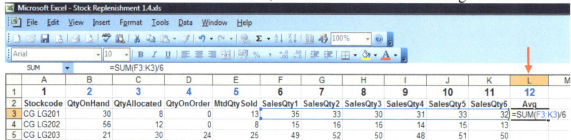

Insert formula in Column G in 'Report' sheet.
And Change 'Avg Run Rate' to Blue font for your easy reference later.

Important:
The VLOOKUP table_array argument now is 'Data!A:L' instead of 'Data!A:K' because the data 'average' which you want to retrieve has been added in Column L in 'Data' sheet OR ELSE an error message #REF!

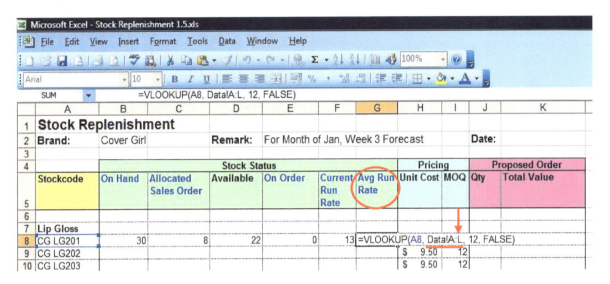

Step 4 – Copy Formula
Copy the formula to all other items' row.

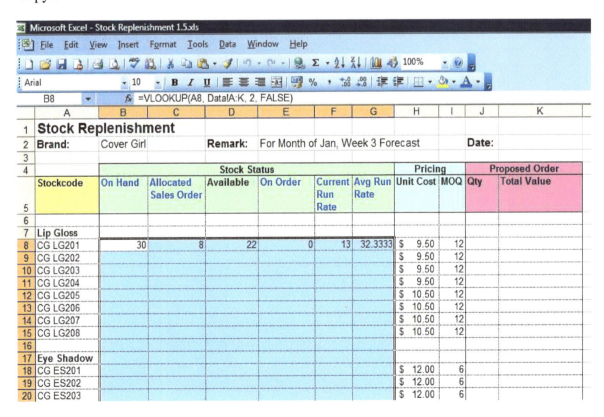

Step 5 – Evaluation

5.1 With all data ready on 'Report' sheet, you can now easily evaluate the inventory & decide the quantity of stocks to replenish.

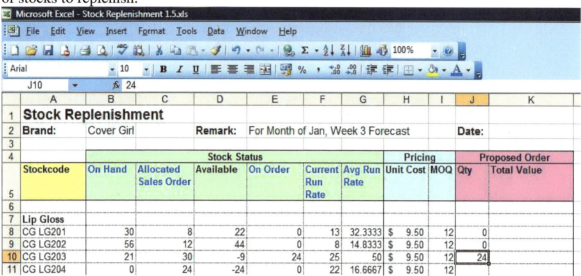

5.2 Lastly, you can insert formula for 'Total Value' in Column K and GRAND TOTAL at cell K31 for your proposed order to check against your purchasing budget.

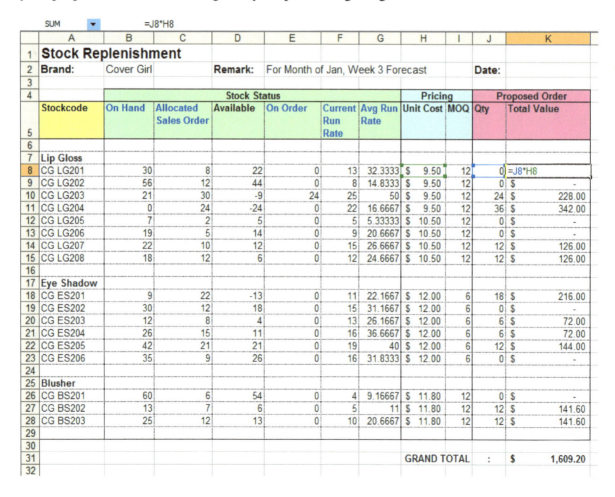

Step 6 – Save Automate Report

The Automate Report is now complete. You can now use this Automate Report to generate the report automatically for you next time just with a few clicks.

Just import the updated data next time in 'Data' sheet, and wait for the data downloading complete. Then you can go to 'Report' sheet to view the report in the formatted way you want.

Note when importing data next time:
- Make sure you place the cursor in cell A2 instead of A1, to keep the Row 1 – Column Number. You can skip the Column Numbering step next time when you're very familiar with this concept. As a starter, you're advice to put the column numbering for your easy reference & avoid confusion.
- You may choose to delete or keep your previous data in Row 2 onwards because the data imported will replace the old data.
- Select the same database table & fields exactly in its order like the first time.
- If you would like to keep every updated report, then save a new file everytime. Eg: The first Automate Report as 'Stock Replenishment Week3.xls' and the next update as 'Stock Replenishment Week4.xls' and so forth.

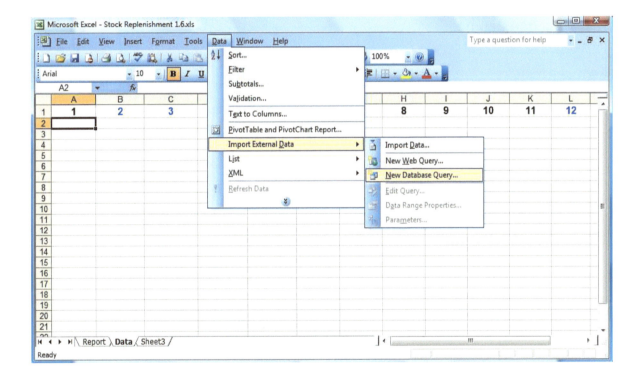

Okay after you have successfully completed this Scenario 1 Automate Report tutorial, you can try to adapt your own scenario in your company to create an Automate Report for yourself & increase your productivity.

4.2 Scenario 2 : Sales Performance Report

Scenario Description

An employee in a principal/vendor company requires to find out the following:
- Monthly sales for a particular brand.
- Update on a weekly basis to monitor customer performance against quota set.
- Sales in units & revenue, for each stockcode & each customer.

Step 1 – Create Report Template

1.3 Open a new excel file & create the report template in Sheet1 OR
   Open the workbook 'Sales Performance 2.0.xls' to continue the tutorial.

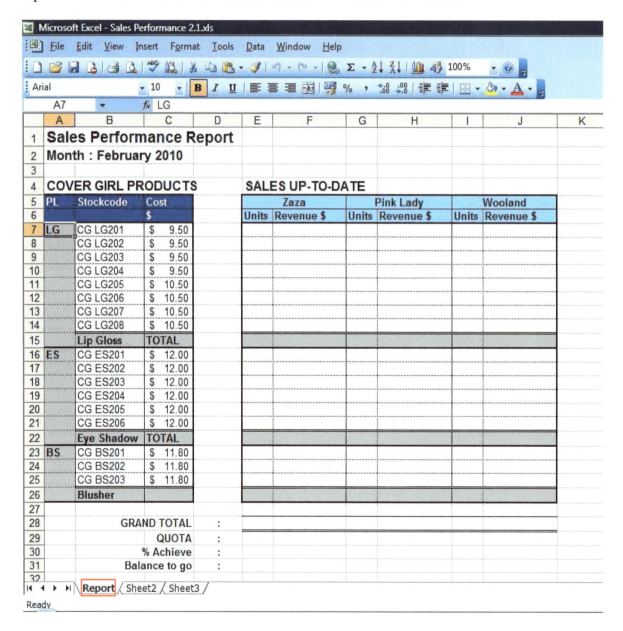

Column A – C
Product/Brand information: Product Line, Stockcode & Cost.

Column E – J
Customer purchase in units & revenue.

Line 28: Total Sales for each customer.

Line 29: Monthly quota set by company for the appointed wholesaler.

Line 30: Percentage achieve by customer.

Line 31: Balance purchase to be made by the customer.

1.4 Rename Sheet1 as 'Report'.

Step 2 – Retrieve Data

2.1 Go to Sheet2 and place your cursor at cell A1 to begin import data / paste the data.
For this scenario, the filtering criteria would be Stockcode for the brand and Date for the month to evaluate.

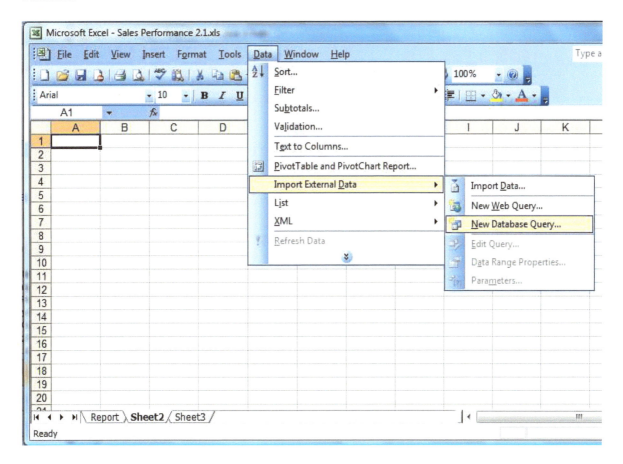

2.2 Rename Sheet2 as 'Data' when data import completed.

For tutorial & learning purpose, the workbook 'Stock Performance 2.0.xls' already contained the below data to simulate the data import completed.

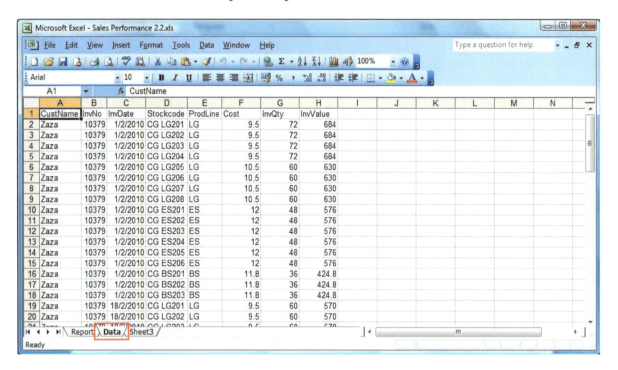

Step 3 – Insert Formula

3.1 Insert a new row at Row 1 in 'Data' sheet and Numbering the columns.

Column G in 'Data' sheet is the data to be retrieved.
While Column A & D are the conditions to retrieve Column G.
Change their font color to Blue to ease you later when inserting formula.

'Data' sheet

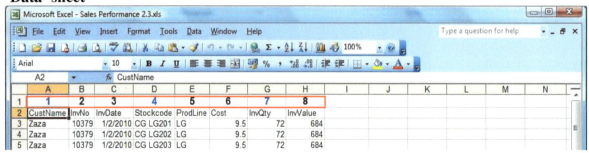

3.2 Go to 'Report' sheet.
   Columns E, G, I in 'Report' sheet are the column to retrieve the data from 'Data' sheet.
   Change the font color to Blue as well for easy reference.

'Report' sheet

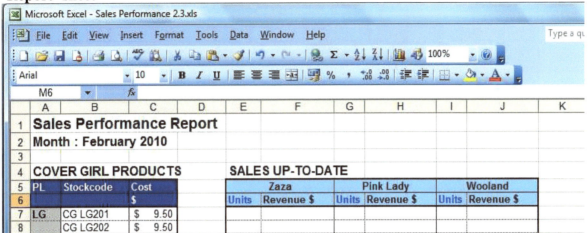

See below table for a better view.

'Report' sheet	Retrieve from	'Data' sheet
[Columns in 'Report' sheet are the columns to retrieve the data from 'Data' sheet. And you can name them what you like.]		[Columns in 'Data' sheet are the columns where the data is imported from a source and to be retrieved to 'Report' sheet. And the columns name appears as what it was named in the database field.]
Column E – Units	=	Column G – InvQty
Column G – Units	=	Column G – InvQty
Column I – Units	=	Column G – InvQty

Table 4.21

3.3 Insert SUM & IF formula.

   3.31 Click on cell E7. Type in as follow:
       =SUM(IF((Data!D1:D100=$B7)*(Data!A1:A100="Zaza"), Data!G1:G100))

Arguments	Description
Data!D1:D100=$B7	Search Column D in 'Data Sheet' from Row 1 to 100 where the items match B7 in 'Report Sheet'.
Data!A1:A100="Zaza"	Search Column A in 'Data Sheet' from Row 1 to 100 where the items match Zaza.
Data!G1:G100	Add the values in Column G from Row 1 to 100 for the rows that match the 2 conditions above.

Table 4.22

Note: For my scenario, I just specify the row up to 100 as my data in 'Data Sheet' is until Row 70 and I would like to make it simple for your learning. To be safe, you can specify the row up to 1,000 or even 10,000 depends on how large your data is. This is to avoid miss out any data that beyond the rows you specify as you might not know how many rows/transactions for the data you import. Excel can store up to 65,535 rows maximum.

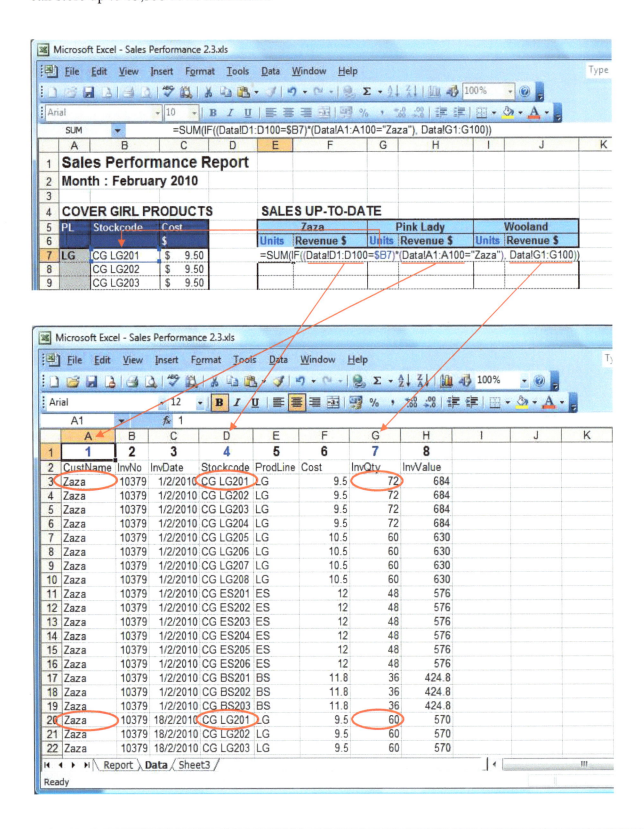

3.32 When the formula complete, press **ENTER** on the keyboard. Press **F2** on keyboard, and then press **CTRL+SHIFT+ENTER** to enter as array formula.

The data is successfully retrieved and shown in cell E7.

Important: The SUM & IF formulas combination must be entered as array formulas. If the formula is not entered as array formula, the error #VALUE! or 0 is returned. When in array formula [enclosed in braces { }], SUM & IF will return 0 too by default if there isn't any record found to be sum.

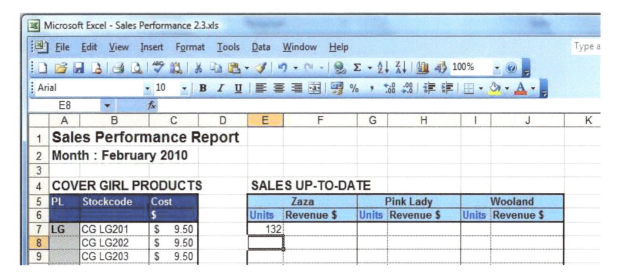

3.33 Repeat Step 3.31 – 3.32 on cell G7 & I7 with the following SUM & IF arguments:

Cell **Formula**
G7   =SUM(IF((Data!D1:D100=$B7)*(Data!A1:A100="Pink Lady"), Data!G1:G100))
I7   =SUM(IF((Data!D1:D100=$B7)*(Data!A1:A100="Wooland"), Data!G1:G100))
Note: Remember to enter as array formula.

The difference of the formula argument is the Customer Name (font highlight in blue above) used to retrieve the data from Column A in 'Data sheet' as explain earlier in Table 4.22.

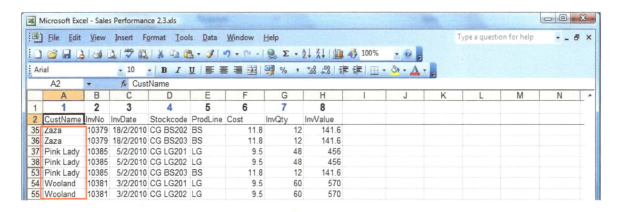

3.4 Insert Other Formula for the remaining columns.

Column	Description
F	Formula: =$C7*E7
H	Formula: =$C7*G7
J	Formula: =$C7*I7
	Well, I guess I do not have to explain much here. The formula above is to compute the revenue for each stockcode for each customer.

Table 4.23

Step 4 – Copy Formula

Copy the formula to all other items' row.

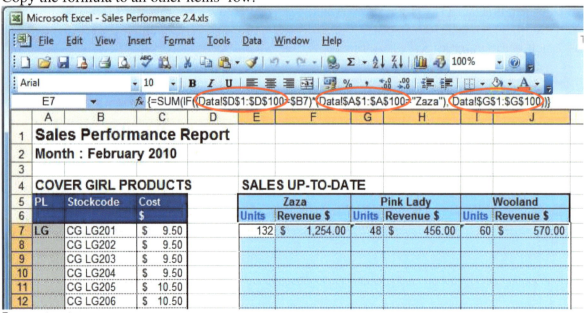

Important:

If you're copying the formula using fill handler / fill down, please add '$' to the data range in the formula in **E7, G7 & I7** to avoid cell addressing change when you copy the formula.

Step 5 – Evaluation

5.1 With all data ready on 'Report' sheet, you can sum up the subtotal & grand total sales for each customer.

	A	B	C	D	E	F	G	H	I	J
1	**Sales Performance Report**									
2	**Month : February 2010**									
3										
4	**COVER GIRL PRODUCTS**				**SALES UP-TO-DATE**					
5	**PL**	**Stockcode**	**Cost**			**Zaza**		**Pink Lady**		**Wooland**
6			**$**		**Units**	**Revenue $**	**Units**	**Revenue $**	**Units**	**Revenue $**
7	LG	CG LG201	$ 9.50		132	$ 1,254.00	48	$ 456.00	60	$ 570.00
8		CG LG202	$ 9.50		132	$ 1,254.00	48	$ 456.00	60	$ 570.00
9		CG LG203	$ 9.50		132	$ 1,254.00	48	$ 456.00	60	$ 570.00
10		CG LG204	$ 9.50		132	$ 1,254.00	48	$ 456.00	60	$ 570.00
11		CG LG205	$ 10.50		108	$ 1,134.00	36	$ 378.00	48	$ 504.00
12		CG LG206	$ 10.50		108	$ 1,134.00	36	$ 378.00	48	$ 504.00
13		CG LG207	$ 10.50		108	$ 1,134.00	36	$ 378.00	48	$ 504.00
14		CG LG208	$ 10.50		108	$ 1,134.00	36	$ 378.00	48	$ 504.00
15		**Lip Gloss**	**TOTAL**		960	$ 9,552.00	336	$ 3,336.00	432	$ 4,296.00
16	ES	CG ES201	$ 12.00		72	$ 864.00	18	$ 216.00	36	$ 432.00
17		CG ES202	$ 12.00		72	$ 864.00	18	$ 216.00	36	$ 432.00
18		CG ES203	$ 12.00		72	$ 864.00	18	$ 216.00	36	$ 432.00
19		CG ES204	$ 12.00		72	$ 864.00	18	$ 216.00	36	$ 432.00
20		CG ES205	$ 12.00		72	$ 864.00	18	$ 216.00	36	$ 432.00
21		CG ES206	$ 12.00		72	$ 864.00	18	$ 216.00	36	$ 432.00
22		**Eye Shadow**	**TOTAL**		432	$ 5,184.00	108	$ 1,296.00	216	$ 2,592.00
23	BS	CG BS201	$ 11.80		48	$ 566.40	12	$ 141.60	24	$ 283.20
24		CG BS202	$ 11.80		48	$ 566.40	12	$ 141.60	24	$ 283.20
25		CG BS203	$ 11.80		48	$ 566.40	12	$ 141.60	24	$ 283.20
26		**Blusher**			144	$ 1,699.20	36	$ 424.80	72	$ 849.60
27										
28		**GRAND TOTAL**	**:**		1536	$ 16,435.20	480	$ 5,056.80	720	$ 7,737.60
29		**QUOTA**	**:**							

5.2 Lastly, insert the 'QUOTA' set for each customer and compute the '%Achieve' & 'Balance to go' to evaluate each customer sales performance against quota.

27									
28	**GRAND TOTAL**	:	1536	$ 16,435.20	480	$ 5,056.80	720	$ 7,737.60	
29	**QUOTA**	:		$ 15,000.00		$ 8,000.00		$ 10,000.00	
30	**% Achieve**	:		109.57%		63.21%		77.38%	
31	**Balance to go**	:		$ (1,435.20)		$ 2,943.20		=J29-J28	
32									

Report / Data / Sheet3 /

Step 6 – Save Automate Report

The Automate Report is now complete. You can now use this Automate Report to generate the report automatically for you next time just with a few clicks.

Just import the updated data next time in 'Data' sheet, and wait for the data downloading complete. Then you can go to 'Report' sheet to view the report in the formatted way you want.

Note when importing data next time:
- Make sure you place the cursor in cell A2 instead of A1, to keep the Row 1 – Column Number. You can skip the Column Numbering step next time when you're very familiar with the concept. As a starter, you're advice to put the column numbering for your easy reference & avoid confusion.
  If you notice, the SUM & IF formula in Scenario 2 did not use the numbering in Row 1 like the VLOOKUP formula in Scenario 1. However, I still insert for the color highlighting purpose for the column we need to refer for your easy reference.
- You may choose to delete or keep your previous data in Row 2 onwards because the data imported will replace the old data.
- Select the same database table & fields exactly in its order like the first time.
- If you would like to keep every updated report, then save a new file everytime. Eg: The first Automate Report as 'Sales Performance Week3.xls' and the next update as 'Sales Performance Week4.xls' and so forth.

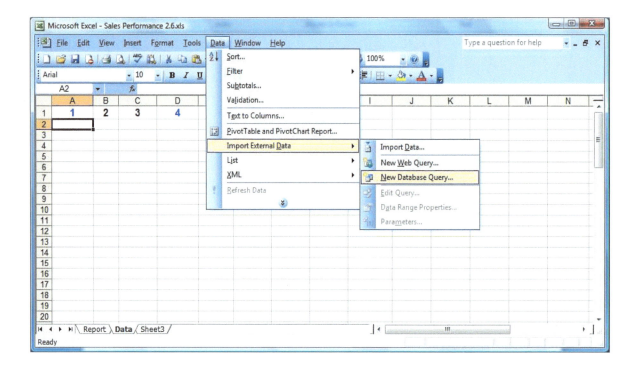

Okay after you have successfully completed this Scenario 2 Automate Report tutorial, you can try to adapt your own similar scenario in your company.

4.3 Scenario 3 : Sales Forecast Report

Scenario Description

An employee in a principal/vendor company requires to forecast sales for a particular brand with the following information:

- Monthly sales for past 3 months.
- Customer's inventory on hand.

Step 1 – Create Report Template

1.1 Open a new excel file & create the report template in Sheet1 OR
    Open the workbook 'Sales Forecast 3.0.xls' to continue the tutorial.

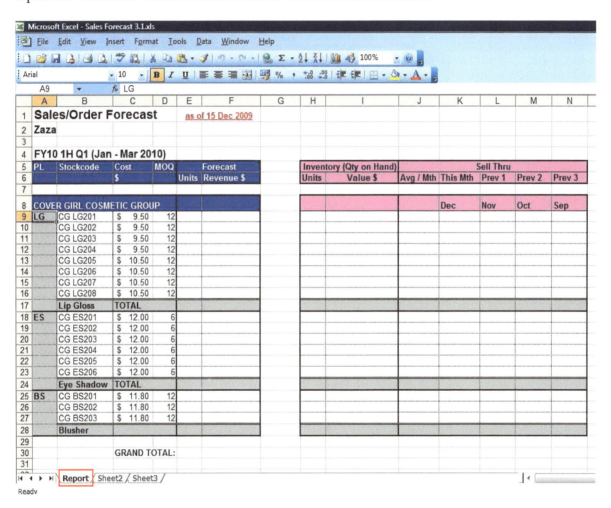

<u>Column A – D</u>
Product/Brand information: Product Line, Stockcode, Cost & MOQ (Min Order Qty)

<u>Column E – F</u>
These are the column for your decision making later at the last part.

<u>Column H – I</u>
Customer's inventory.

Column J – N
Customer's sales record which to be retrieved from *Raw Data / Database*.

Line 30: Total Forecast / Sales.

1.2 Rename Sheet1 as 'Report'.

1.3 Often, most customers system is not connected to the Principal/Vendor. Only a few big multi-national companies do where they invest a lot in the system. Usually for most that do not, the employees have to get back the data from their customers.

For this Scenario 3, it is required to gather customers' inventory from customer.
Create a template to get the customer's inventory.

Open a new excel file & create the inventory template in Sheet1 as shown below OR
Open the workbook 'Inventory CG.xls' to continue the tutorial.

Once template had been created, send to customers to fill in their respective column. Assuming the file has been sent. While waiting for customer's response, let's continue on retrieving the customer's sales record from database.

Step 2 – Retrieve Data

2.1 Go to Sheet2 and place your cursor at cell A1 to begin import data / paste the data. For this scenario, the filtering criteria would be Stockcode for the brand & month range.

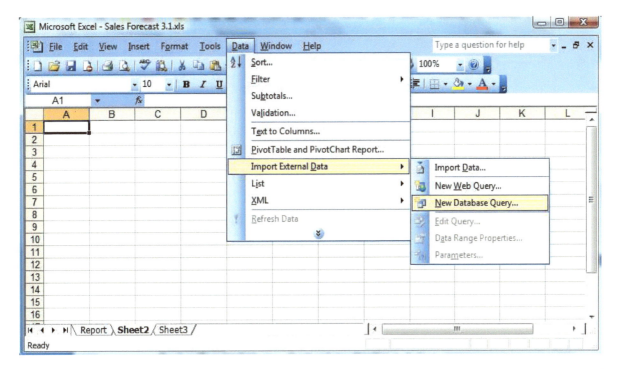

2.2 Rename Sheet2 as 'ST' (represents Sell Thru) when data import completed.

For tutorial & learning purpose, the workbook 'Sales Forecast 3.0.xls' already contained the below data to simulate the data import completed.

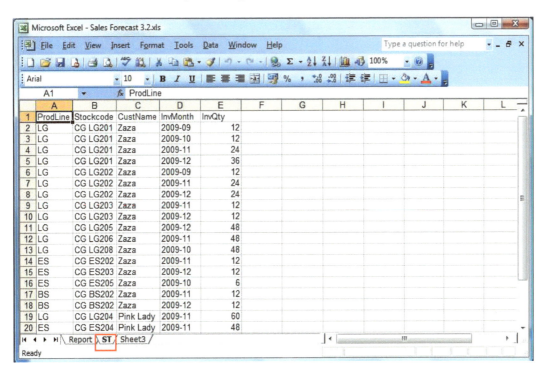

2.3 Now, the data from system has been retrieved. Let's move to the data that need to be gathered from customers, which is inventory.

Open the Inventory Report template 'Inventory CG.xls' > Right Click on Sheet1 > Select Move or Copy.

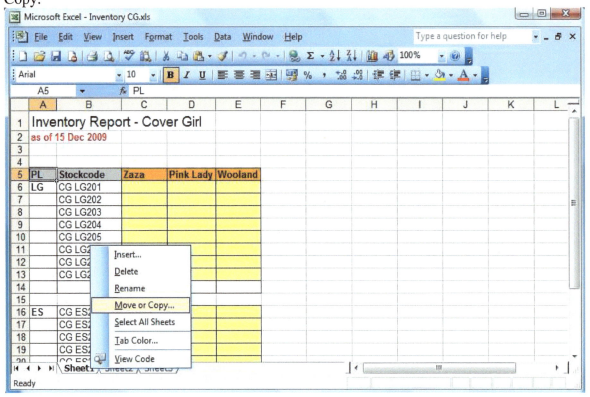

'Move or Copy' window appeared > Click on 'To book:' drop-down box > Select 'Sales Forecast 3.0.xls'. Then in 'Before sheet:' list box select 'Sheet3' and Tick 'Create a copy' tick box.

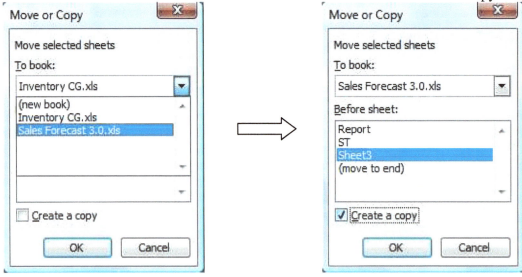

2.4 Assuming all customers have reverted on the Inventory Report and the report is saved under 3 different files name. For tutorial & learning purpose, the 'Workbook-ExcelAutomateReport' folder (refer to Page 23) contained the above mentioned files to simulate the scenario.

Open 'Inventory CG - Zaza.xls'.
Select the filled cell and Copy the cell to 'Sales Forecast Report' > 'Inventory' sheet.

Inventory Report from Customers   **Sales Forecast Report - Inventory sheet**

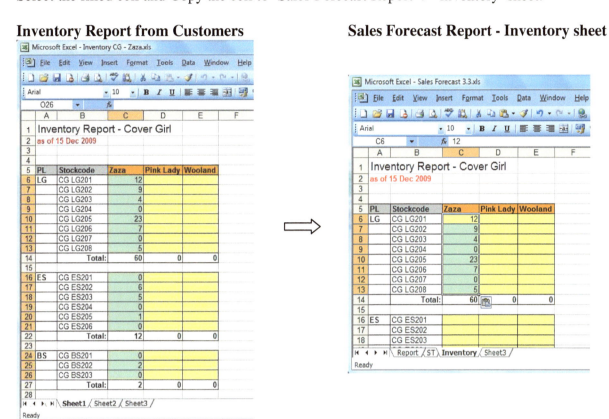

Open 'Inventory CG – Pink Lady.xls' & 'Inventory CG – Wooland.xls' and repeat the same to copy all customer's inventory to 'Sales Forecast Report' > 'Inventory' sheet.

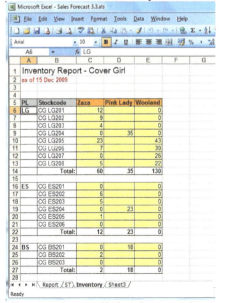

Now we have all the data ready, and let's move to next step: Insert Formula.

Step 3 – Insert Formula

3.1 Insert VLOOKUP formula.

As explained earlier in Chapter 2 under 2.2 Big 5 Formulas, VLOOKUP function is designed to search the value in the first column of table array. In other words, if the search item is not in the first column, VLOOKUP can't find the value and returned error.

Here, I will teach you how to combine VLOOKUP & DEFINE NAME formula to perform such search where the first column is not the search item's column.

For instance, like the inventory template created for customer, sometime we have certain format to adhere, to make it neat and formal to customer instead of sending a database format to customer.

The inventory template first column (column A) is PL instead of the search item's column 'Stockcode'.

3.11 Select Column B, C, D & E on 'Inventory' sheet in Sales Forecast file.
Click Insert > Name > Define.

'Inventory' sheet

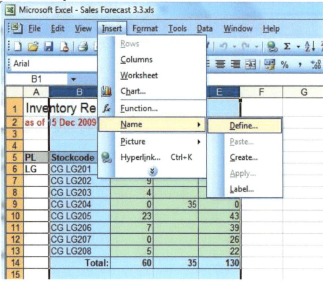

3.12 'Define Name' window appeared.
Type 'INV' on the 'Names in workbook' textbox > Click OK.

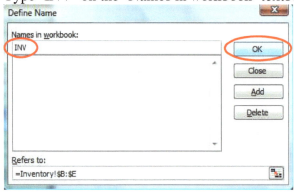

To confirm you have defined name correctly, highlight Column B to E again and check the name box show 'INV'. If it doesn't show 'INV', means you didn't define the name correctly and there will be error occurred when insert VLOOKUP formula later. You may have to re-define the name until you get it right.

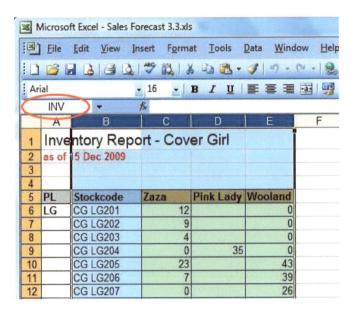

3.13 Numbering the column at Row 4.

Columns C, D, E are the data to be retrieved.

Change their font color to Blue for easy reference when inserting formula.

3.14 Go to 'Report' sheet. Please take note that this report is for Customer Zaza.
Columns H, K, L, M & N are the data to be retrieved.
Change their font color to Blue for easy reference when inserting formula.

'Report' sheet

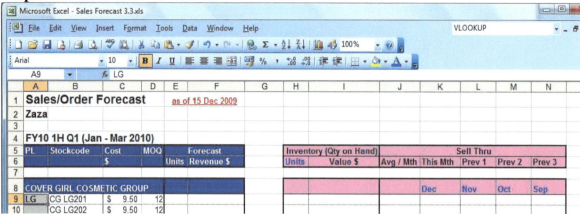

See below table for a better view.

'Report' sheet	Retrieve from	'Inventory' sheet
Column H – Units	=	Column C – Zaza

'Report' sheet		'ST' sheet
Column K – Dec	=	Column E – InvQty
Column L – Nov	=	Column E – InvQty
Column M – Oct	=	Column E – InvQty
Column N – Sep	=	Column E – InvQty

Table 4.31

3.15 Click on cell H9. Type in as follow:
=VLOOKUP($B9,INV, 2, FALSE)

Arguments	Description
$B9	The item that you want to search.
INV	Where your data is placed. The VLOOKUP will search the 'INV' table array where we have defined Column B to E in 'Inventory' sheet as INV earlier. In other word, VLOOKUP will search the 'Inventory' sheet from Column B to E for a match to the item in A8.
2	Which column's value to return from INV table array when VLOOKUP find a match. The 'Inventory for Zaza' is in Column No. 2 in 'INV' table array. **Important:** As 'INV' table array refer to 'Inventory' sheet Column B to E, therefore Column B is column number 1 instead of column number 2 as numbered at Step 3.33. Follow by Column C as column number 2.
FALSE	To find an exact match only. So that you know if an error value #N/A is displayed, there isn't such records from the data you imported.

Table 4.32

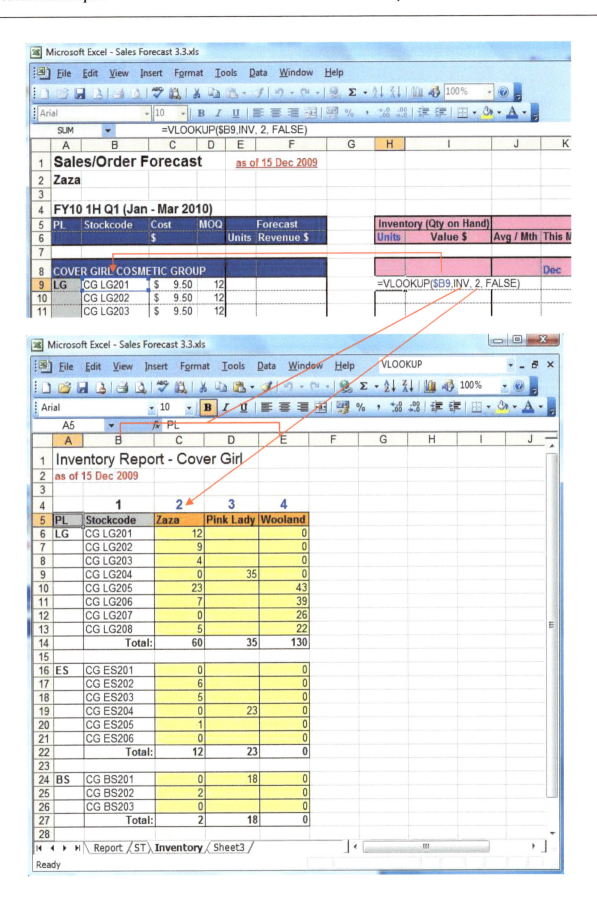

3.16 When the formula complete, press **ENTER** on the keyboard.
The data is successfully retrieved and shown in cell H9.

Note: If error value #N/A is displayed, it means in the data you imported do not have the item record you're searching for. To get rid of the error value #N/A, combine VLOOKUP & ISERROR formula which taught in Chapter 2 under 2.2 - *Big 5 formulas*.

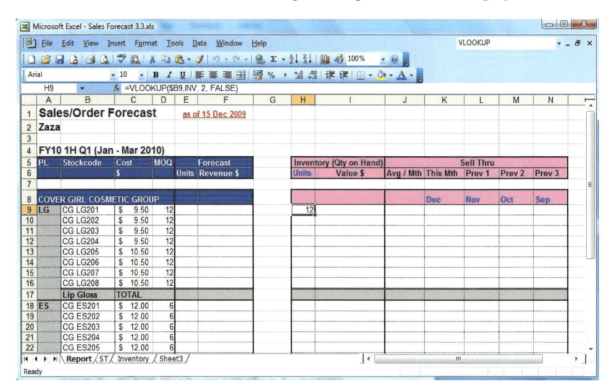

3.2 Insert SUM & IF formula.

3.21 Go to 'ST' sheet.
Column E in 'ST' sheet is the data to be retrieved.
While Columns B, C & D are the conditions to retrieve Column E.
Change their font color to Blue to ease you later when inserting formula.

If you recall in, in Scenario 2 I have explained at the last page on the Note: point no.1, that SUM & IF formula do not use numbering in the formula like VLOOKUP. Therefore, you can directly highlight the FieldName instead of insert a numbering row.

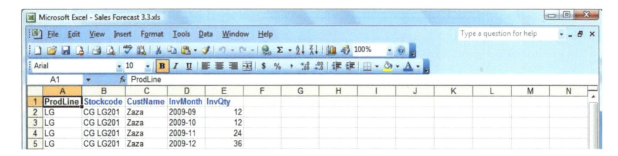

3.22 Go to 'Report' sheet. Click on cell K10. Type in as follow:
=SUM(IF((ST!$B$1:$B$100=$B9)*(ST!$C$1:$C$100="Zaza")*(ST!$D$1:$D$100="2009-12"), ST!$E$1:$E$100))

Arguments	Description
ST!$B$1:$B$100=$B9	Search Column B in 'ST Sheet' from Row 1 to 100 where the items match B9.
ST!$C$1:$C$100="Zaza"	Search Column C in 'ST Sheet' from Row 1 to 100 where the items match Zaza.
ST!$D$1:$D$100="2009-12"	Search Column D in 'ST Sheet' from Row 1 to 100 where the items match 2009-12.
ST!$E$1:$E$100	Add the values in Column E from Row 1 to 100 for the rows that match the 3 conditions above.

Table 4.32

Note: As explained earlier in Scenario 2, I just specify the row up to 100 to make it simple for your learning. You can specify the row up to 1,000 or even 10,000 depends on how large your data is. Excel can store up to 65,535 rows maximum. Also, adding of '$' to the formula is to avoid cell addressing change when you copy the formula.

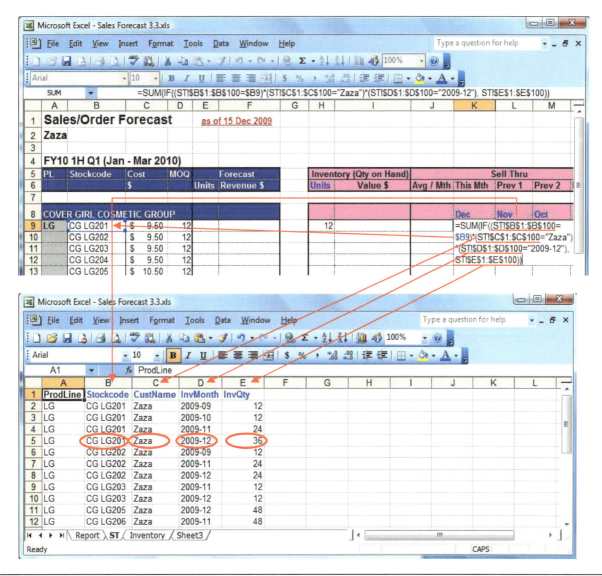

3.23 When the formula complete, press **ENTER** on the keyboard. Press **F2** on keyboard, and then press **CTRL+SHIFT+ENTER** to enter as array formula.

The data is successfully retrieved and shown in cell K10.

Important: The SUM & IF formulas combination must be entered as array formulas. If the formula is not entered as array formula, the error #VALUE! or 0 is returned. When in array formula [enclosed in braces { }], SUM & IF will return 0 too by default if there isn't any record found to be sum.

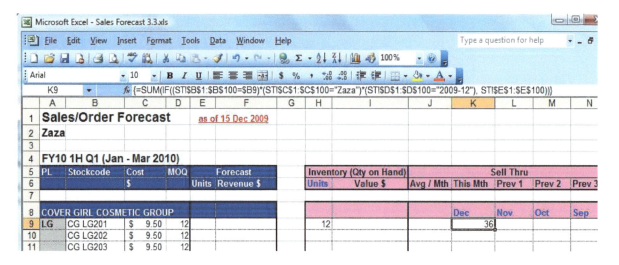

3.24 Repeat Step 3.22 – 3.23 on cell L10, M10 & N10 with the following SUM & IF arguments:

Cell	Formula
L10	=SUM(IF((ST!$B$1:$B$100=$B9)*(ST!$C$1:$C$100="Zaza")*(ST!$D$1:$D$100="2009-11"), ST!$E$1:$E$100))
M10	=SUM(IF((ST!$B$1:$B$100=$B9)*(ST!$C$1:$C$100="Zaza")*(ST!$D$1:$D$100="2009-10"), ST!$E$1:$E$100))
N10	=SUM(IF((ST!$B$1:$B$100=$B9)*(ST!$C$1:$C$100="Zaza")*(ST!$D$1:$D$100="2009-09"), ST!$E$1:$E$100))

Note: Remember to enter as array formula.

The difference of the formula argument is the Month (font highlight in blue above) used to retrieve the data from Column D in 'ST sheet' as explain earlier in Table 4.32.

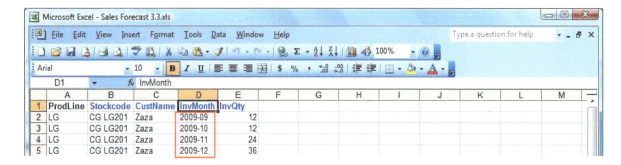

3.3 Insert Other Formula for the remaining columns.

Column	Description	Explanation
F	Formula: =$E9*$C9	To compute forecast revenue
I	Formula: =$H9*$C9	To compute inventory on hand value
J	Formula: =(L9+M9+N9)/3	To compute past 3 months average sales/mth

Table 4.33

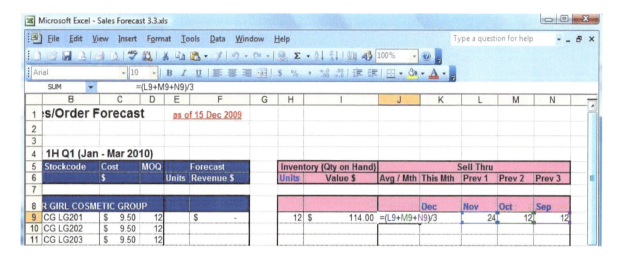

Step 4 – Copy Formula

Copy the formula to all other items' row.

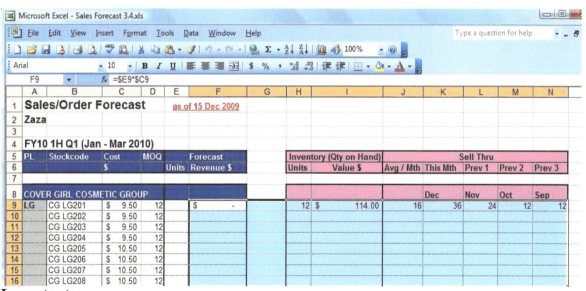

Important:

Please take note of the cell addressing if you did not use or miss out the '$' in the formula when you copy the formula using fill handler / fill down.

Step 5 – Evaluation

5.1 After complete copy all formula for each items' row, you can now sum up the subtotal & grand total for forecast, inventory & sales history for customer Zaza.

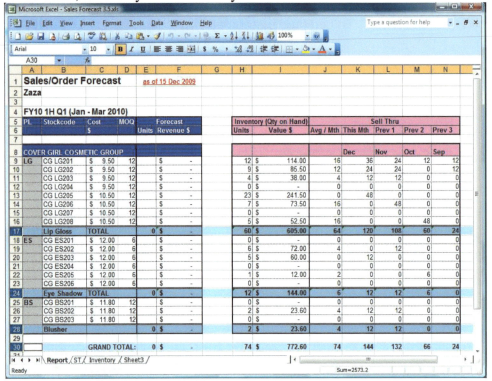

5.2 Lastly, with all data ready on Report' sheet, you can now evaluate the customer's sales history plus inventory on hand to make more accurate forecast of the coming quarter's sales to be committed by this customer Zaza.

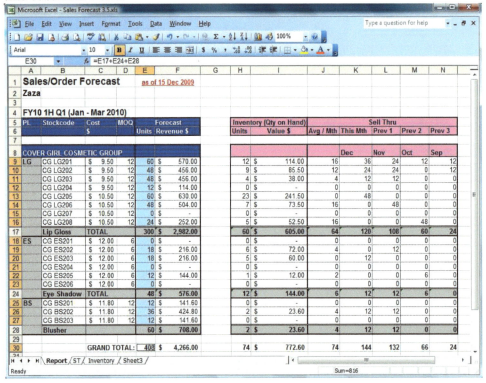

5.3 We have done the report for customer Zaza. We can now repeat the same report for other customer. Rename 'Report' sheet to 'Rpt Zaza'.

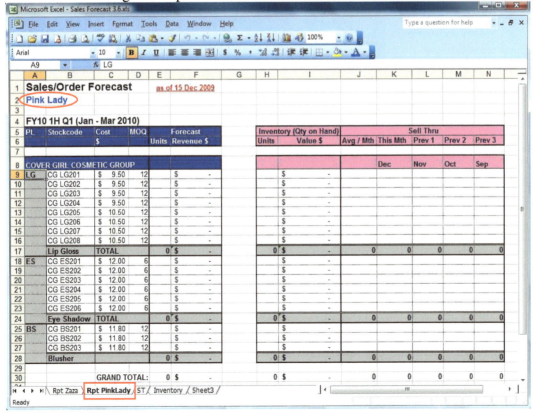

5.4 Insert a new sheet, rename as 'Rpt PinkLady' & copy the template from Rpt Zaza. Remember to change the report title as well.

5.5 Insert VLOOKUP formula for customer Pink Lady. Click on cell H9. Type in as follow:
=VLOOKUP($B9,INV, 3, FALSE)

The difference in the formula compare to the earlier report for customer Zaza is the column number which is 3 as highlight in blue above.

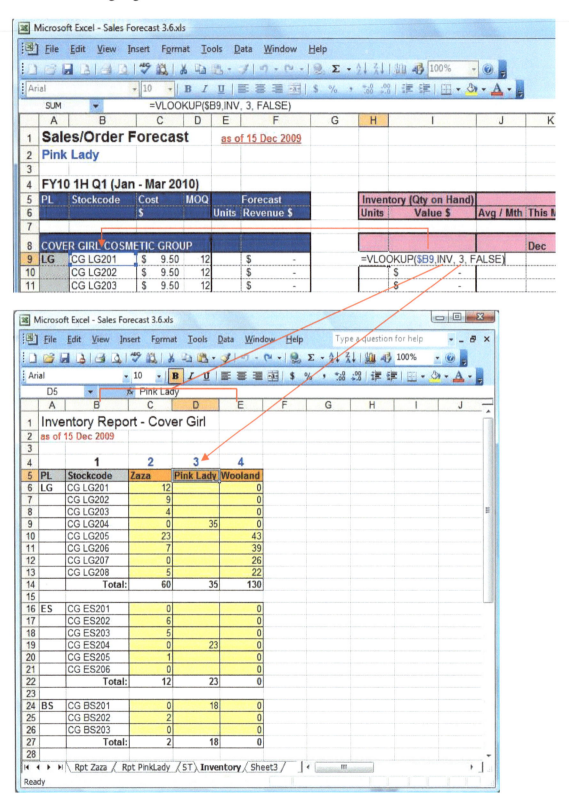

5.6 Insert SUM & IF formula for customer Pink Lady. Click on cell K10. Type in as follow:
=SUM(IF((ST!$B$1:$B$100=$B9)*(ST!$C$1:$C$100="Pink Lady")*(ST!$D$1:$D$100="2009-12"), ST!$E$1:$E$100))

The difference in the formula compare to the earlier report for customer Zaza is the customer name which we retrieved from Column C in 'ST sheet' as highlight in blue above.

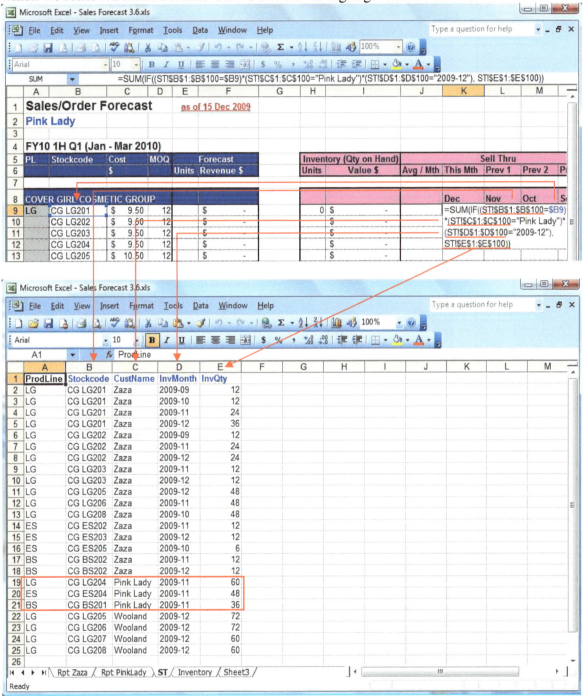

When the formula complete, press **ENTER** on the keyboard. Press **F2** on keyboard, and then press **CTRL+SHIFT+ENTER** to enter as array formula.

5.7 Repeat Step 3.33 to Step 5.2 to complete the report for customer Pink Lady.

Important:
When you repeat the steps, remember to change the 2nd condition to "Pink Lady" as well.

Note:
There will be only 3 records retrieved as the database imported only contained 3 Pink Lady transactions as highlighted in previous page.

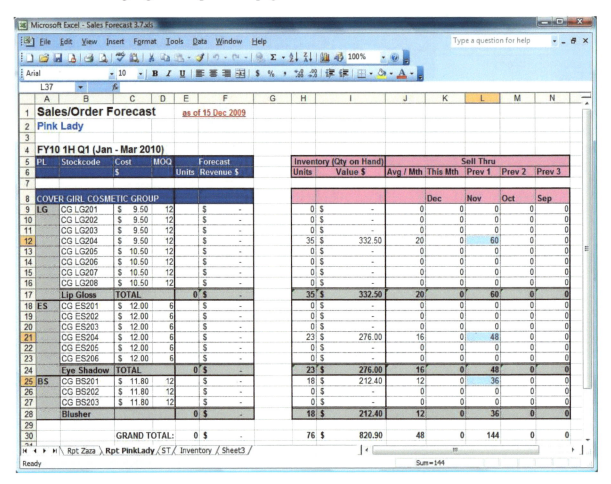

5.8 You can try another report for customer Wooland by repeat Step 3.33 to Step 5.2 again. The keyword this time to be change is "Wooland" in 2nd condition, as how the customer name appeared in database imported.

To check whether you have successfully retrieved the data for Wooland, the sales history should show 4 records only as per data in 'ST sheet'.

Step 6 – Save Automate Report

The Automate Report is now complete. You can now use this Automate Report to generate the report automatically for you next time just with a few clicks.

Usually for forecasting, employee is required to do quite a number of times when next quarter is around the corner until the plan is approved by management.

With ExcelAutomateReport, you can just import the updated data next time in 'ST' sheet, and also get the customer inventory with inventory template and copy it to the 'Inventory' sheet.

Then you can go to as many customer report sheet 'Rpt CustName' to view the report in the formatted way you want without go through the tedious report making process like ever before.

Note when importing data next time:
- In this scenario, we have skipped to insert the numbering at Row 1 as SUM & IF formula do not use numbering in the formula like VLOOKUP as explained earlier, make sure you place the cursor in cell A1 instead of cell A2.
- You may choose to delete or keep your previous data in Row 1 onwards because the data imported will replace the old data.
- Select the same database table & fields exactly in its order like the first time.
- If you would like to keep every updated report, then save a new file everytime. Eg: The first Automate Report as 'Sales Forecast v1.xls' and the next update as 'Sales Forecast v2.xls' and so forth.

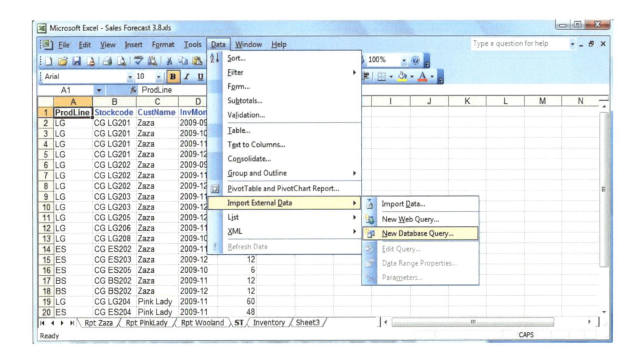

Okay after you have successfully completed this Scenario 3 Automate Report tutorial, you can try to adapt your own similar scenario in your company.

4.4 Scenario 4 : Product Performance Analysis

Scenario Description

A principal/vendor company with headquarter office & factory overseas have several sales & marketing office in other countries.

These branches are responsible for sales & distribution to the local market where they appoint several distributors as the main wholesaler. The distributors (tier-2 customers) are then re-selling the stocks to smaller dealers (tier-3 customers).

The branches will collect sales from local market and the HQ factory will ship out the goods to their customers directly. The admin clerk in local office will get a copy of the documentation (Invoice, DO etc) from the factory.

None of this sales information is available to be viewed or retrieved from a computer system as the branches do not have ERP/SAP system. The admin clerk is required to do the record keeping in a worksheet for the Sales Manager.

Beside the detail monthly sales to customers, the admin clerk is required to prepare an analysis of sales by product category & product line every quarter for the Sales Manager to understand their customers' sales channel.

Step 1 – Create Report Template

1.1 Open a new excel file & create the report template in Sheet1 OR
Open the workbook 'Product Performance 4.0.xls' to continue the tutorial.

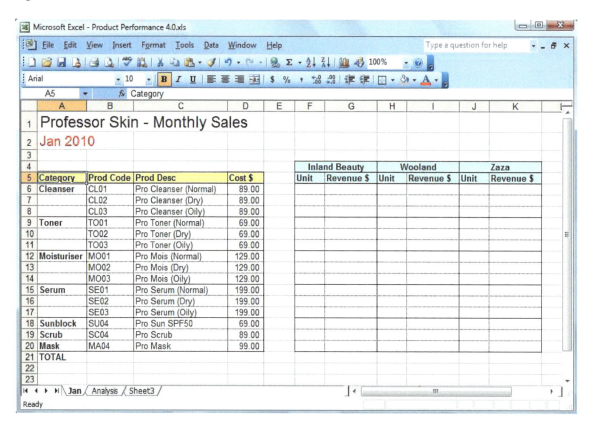

There are 2 type of report template involved in this scenario here:
1. Monthly Sales Report template – 'Jan' sheet.
2. Quarterly Analysis of Product Sales Performance – 'Analysis' sheet.

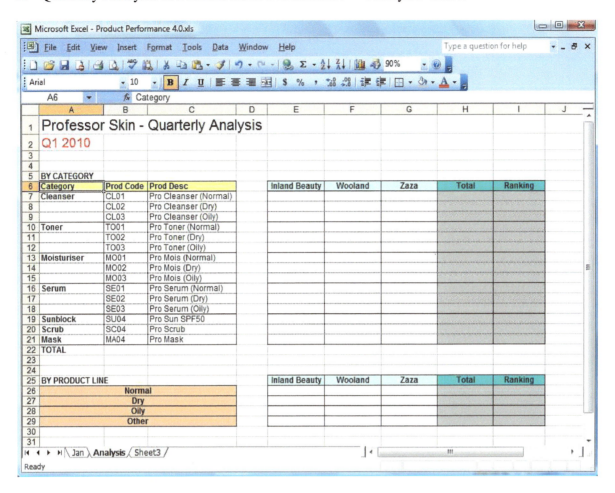

Step 2 – Retrieve Data

2.1 For this scenario, as information is not available to be imported from a system, it is best to enter the data into the spreadsheet in database format as explained in Chapter 2 Data.

Go to 'Sheet3', create the following field name as per Invoice/DO and enter to Sheet 3:

1. InvNo
2. InvDate
3. InvMonth
4. CustNo
5. CustName
6. ProdCode
7. ProdDesc
8. Category
9. PL
10. InvQty
11. InvValue

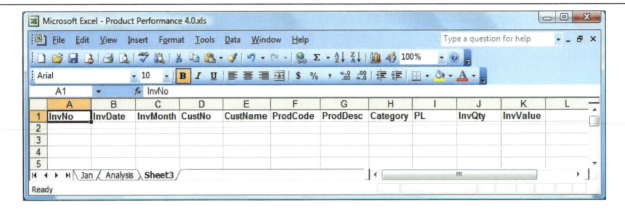

Note:

When creating the field name for the database in spreadsheet yourself, beside follow what stated in the Invoice document, you have to think what data field to be added or omit from the Invoice.

In this scenario, the following data field has been added or omitted:

- **InvMonth** – added to identify which month the sales fall into as date itself can only be use to sum daily sales and not monthly sales.
- **Category & PL** – added to be use in analysis for evaluation of product performance
- **UnitPrice** – omitted as it will be more flexible to be entered on template and compute the value using formula. However, the InvValue is entered in the database because it will be easier if you want to refer to a particular transaction in spreadsheet instead of digging back the stack of files when the management or customer ask to check.

Invoice document received by local office / admin clerk

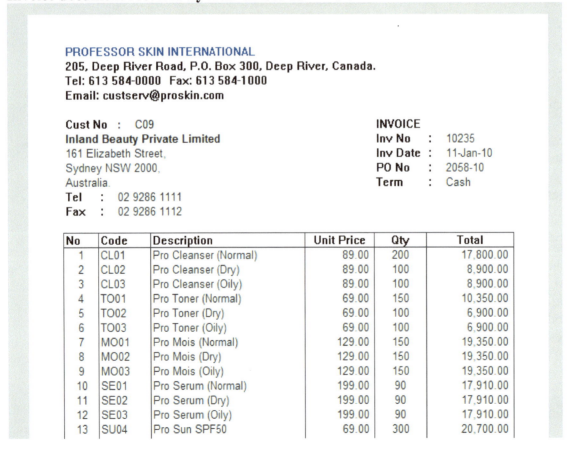

2.2 Now, the data field had been identified & created. Data entry job begin here ... enter the data for each transaction one by one.

For tutorial & learning purpose, the workbook 'Database.xls' already contained the data to simulate the admin clerk already entered all customers purchase for the quarter (Jan-Mar 2010).

Copy all the data from 'Database.xls' workbook to Sheet3 & rename it as 'Data'.

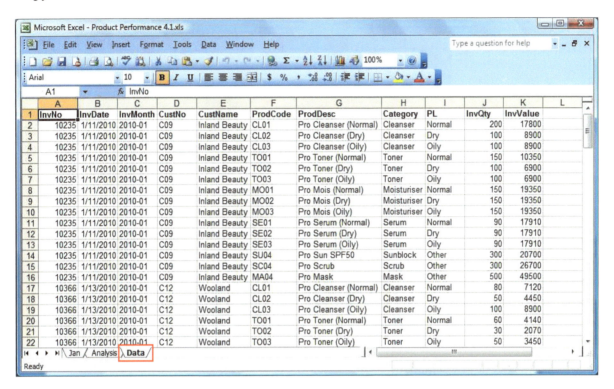

Step 3 – Insert Formula

3.1 Insert SUM & IF formula for **'Monthly Sales Report Template'**.

3.11 Go to 'Data' sheet.
   Column J in 'Data' sheet is the data to be retrieved.
   While Columns C, D & F are the conditions to retrieve Column J.
   Change their font color to Blue to ease you later when inserting formula.

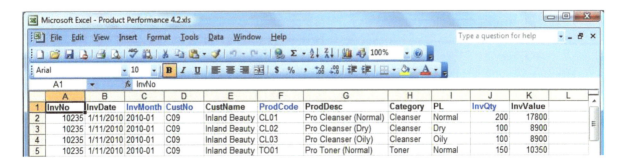

3.12 Go to 'Jan' sheet.

Columns F, H & J in 'Report' sheet are the column to retrieve the data from 'Data' sheet. Change the font color to Blue as well for easy reference.

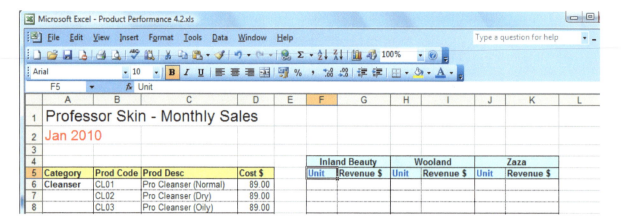

See below table for a better view.

'Jan' sheet	Retrieve from	'Data' sheet
Column F – Unit	=	Column J – InvQty
Column H – Unit	=	Column J – InvQty
Column J – Unit	=	Column J – InvQty

Table 4.41

This monthly sales report template formula concept is similar with Scenario 2. The only differences are:

- CustNo Field (C09, C12 & C22)

  When CustNo field is available, it is better to use CustNo instead of CustName as CustNo usually shorter and do not have spacing like CustName

- InvMonth Field (2010-01, 2010-02 & 2010-03)

  Scenario 4 involve InvMonth field as the data require to store in 'Data' Sheet is from different month to prepare the quarterly report (as explained earlier at Step 2.1 the InvMonth field is use to identify which month the sales fall into) while Scenario 2 data is filtered by date to import/store only data within a particular month to prepare the monthly report.

- Search Range up to Row 1000

  For this scenario, I specified up to 1000 as 3 months data is usually huge and will exceed 100 rows definitely.

'Jan' Sheet

Cell   Formula

F6   =SUM(IF((Data!$F$1:$F$1000=$B6)*(Data!$D$1:$D$1000="C09")
        *(Data!$C$1:$C$1000="2010-01"), Data!$J$1:$J$1000))

H6   =SUM(IF((Data!$F$1:$F$1000=$B6)*(Data!$D$1:$D$1000="C12")
        *(Data!$C$1:$C$1000="2010-01"), Data!$J$1:$J$1000))

I6   =SUM(IF((Data!$F$1:$F$1000=$B6)*(Data!$D$1:$D$1000="C22")
        *(Data!$C$1:$C$1000="2010-01"), Data!$J$1:$J$1000))

Note: Remember to enter as array formula.

3.13 Complete the monthly sales report for Jan, Feb & Mar. (assuming Quarter 1 ended)
The formula difference this time from Jan report to Feb & Mar report is the month value (2010-01, 2010-02 & 2010-03).

'Feb' Sheet

Cell	Formula
F6	=SUM(IF((Data!$F$1:$F$1000=$B6)*(Data!$D$1:$D$1000="C09")*(Data!$C$1:$C$1000="2010-02"), Data!$J$1:$J$1000))
H6	=SUM(IF((Data!$F$1:$F$1000=$B6)*(Data!$D$1:$D$1000="C12")*(Data!$C$1:$C$1000="2010-02"), Data!$J$1:$J$1000))
I6	=SUM(IF((Data!$F$1:$F$1000=$B6)*(Data!$D$1:$D$1000="C22")*(Data!$C$1:$C$1000="2010-02"), Data!$J$1:$J$1000))

'Mar' Sheet

Cell	Formula
F6	=SUM(IF((Data!$F$1:$F$1000=$B6)*(Data!$D$1:$D$1000="C09")*(Data!$C$1:$C$1000="2010-03"), Data!$J$1:$J$1000))
H6	=SUM(IF((Data!$F$1:$F$1000=$B6)*(Data!$D$1:$D$1000="C12")*(Data!$C$1:$C$1000="2010-03"), Data!$J$1:$J$1000))
I6	=SUM(IF((Data!$F$1:$F$1000=$B6)*(Data!$D$1:$D$1000="C22")*(Data!$C$1:$C$1000="2010-03"), Data!$J$1:$J$1000))

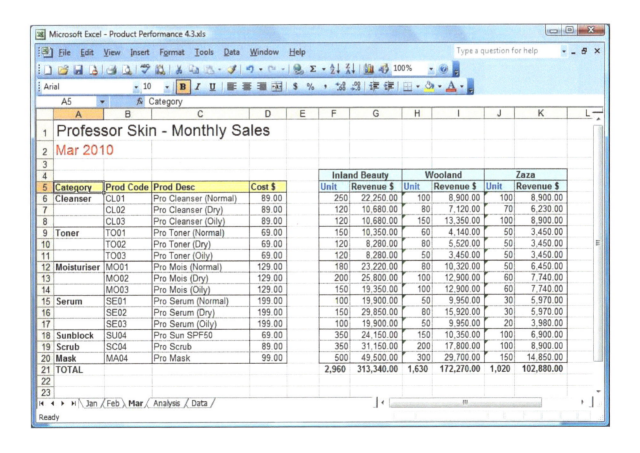

3.2 Insert SUM & IF formula for *'Analysis Report Template'*.

As the quarter already comes to an end, it is time for the admin clerk to prepare the analysis report.

3.21 Go to 'Data' sheet.
Column K in 'Data' sheet is the data to be retrieved.
While Columns D & I are the conditions to retrieve Column K.
Highlight the column Yellow to ease you later when inserting formula.

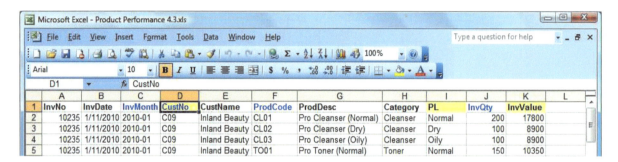

3.22 Go to 'Analysis' sheet.
Columns E, F & G (Row 26-29 only) in 'Analysis' sheet is the column to retrieve the data from 'Data' sheet. Change the font color of E25, F25 & G25 to Blue as well for easy reference.

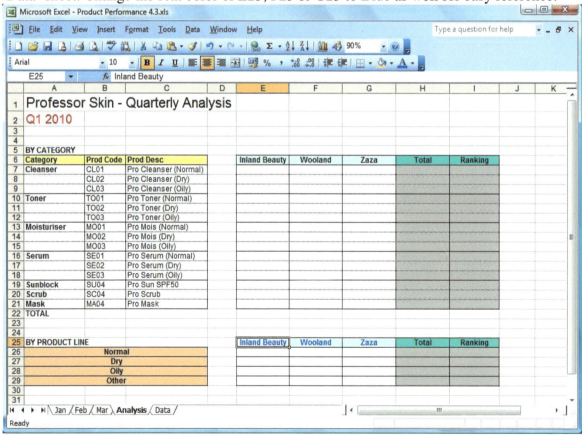

See below table for a better view.

'Analysis' sheet	Retrieve from	'Data' sheet
Column E – Unit	=	Column K – InvValue
Column F – Unit	=	Column K – InvValue
Column G – Unit	=	Column K – InvValue

Table 4.42

3.23 Click on cell E26. Type in as follow:
=SUM(IF((Data!$I$1:$I$1000=$A26)*(Data!$D$1:$D$1000="C09"), Data!$K$1:$K$1000))

Arguments	Description
Data!$I$1:$I$1000=$A26	Search Column I in 'Data Sheet' from Row 1 to 1000 where the items match A26 in 'Analysis Sheet'.
Data!$D$1:$D$1000="C09"	Search Column D in 'Data Sheet' from Row 1 to 1000 where the items match C09.
Data!$K$1:$K$1000	Add the values in Column K from Row 1 to 1000 for the rows that match the 2 conditions above.

Table 4.43
Note: Remember to enter as array formula.

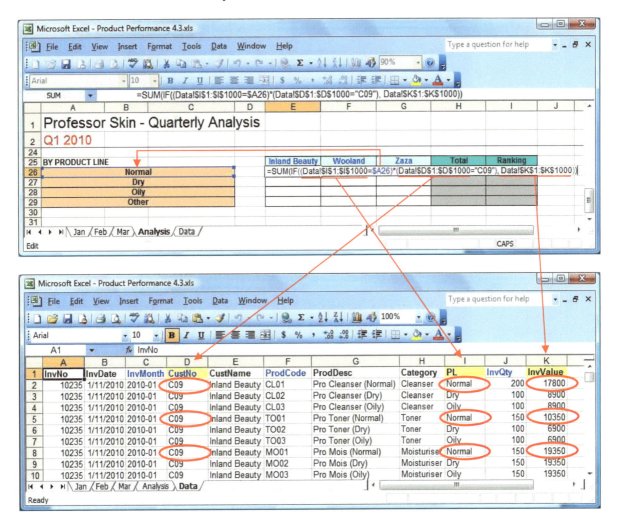

3.24 When the formula complete, press **ENTER** on the keyboard. Press **F2** on keyboard, and then press **CTRL+SHIFT+ENTER** to enter as array formula.

The data is successfully retrieved and shown in cell E26.

Important: The SUM & IF formulas combination must be entered as array formulas. If the formula is not entered as array formula, the error #VALUE! or 0 is returned. When in array formula [enclosed in braces { }], SUM & IF will return 0 too by default if there isn't any record found to be sum.

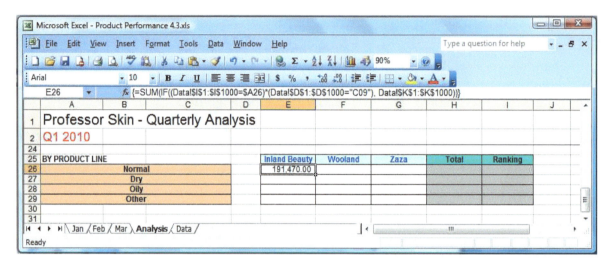

3.25 Repeat Step 3.23 - 3.24 on cell F26 & F27 with the following SUM & IF arguments:

Cell	Formula
F26	=SUM(IF((Data!$I$1:$I$1000=$A26)*(Data!$D$1:$D$1000="C12"), Data!$K$1:$K$1000))
G27	=SUM(IF((Data!$I$1:$I$1000=$A26)*(Data!$D$1:$D$1000="C22"), Data!$K$1:$K$1000))

Note: Remember to enter as array formula.

The difference of the formula argument is the Customer No (font highlight in blue above) used to retrieve the data from Column D in 'Data sheet' as explain earlier in Table 4.43.

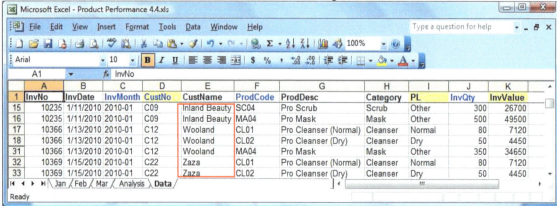

3.3 Insert Other Formula for the remaining cells in 'Analysis' sheet.

Cell	Formula	Explanation
E7	=Jan!G6+Feb!G6+Mar!G6	To compute revenue generated from each product for each customer.
F7	=Jan!I6+Feb!I6+Mar!I6	
G7	=Jan!K6+Feb!K6+Mar!K6	

Table 4.44

Note:
You may also use SUM & IF formula here but since we already compute them in individual *'Monthly Sales Report Template'*, it is easier to just add them from 'Jan', 'Feb' & 'Mar' sheet.

'Analysis' sheet

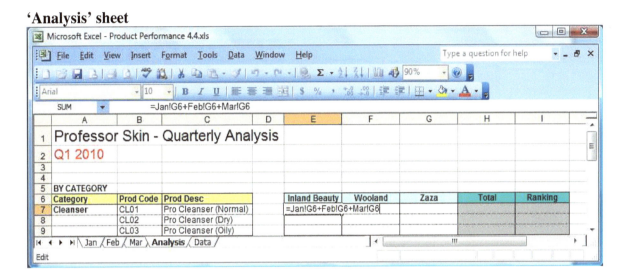

Tips:
Instead of typing the formula, you can click on Cell E7, press = on keyboard,

then click on 'Jan' sheet, select cell G6, press + on keyboard,

then click on 'Feb' sheet, select cell G6, press + on keyboard,

then click on 'Mar' sheet, select cell G6, press + on keyboard,

AND press **ENTER** on the keyboard to achieve the formula.

'Jan' sheet

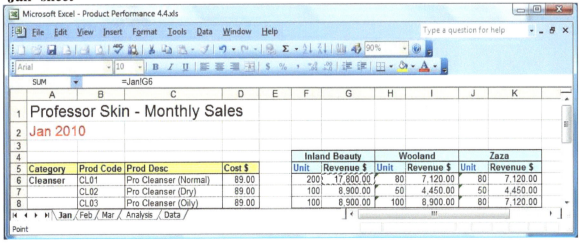

'Feb' sheet

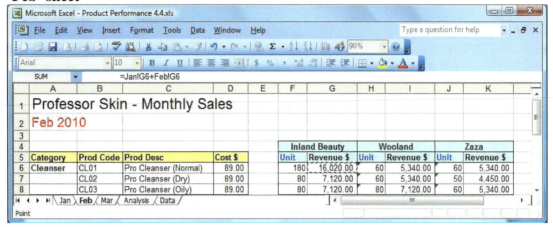

'Mar' sheet

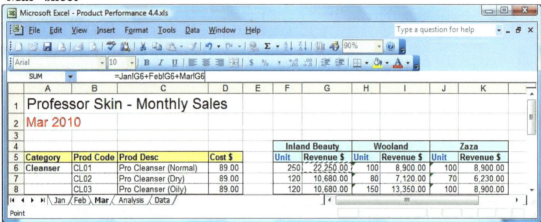

Step 4 – Copy Formula
Copy the formula to all other items' row.

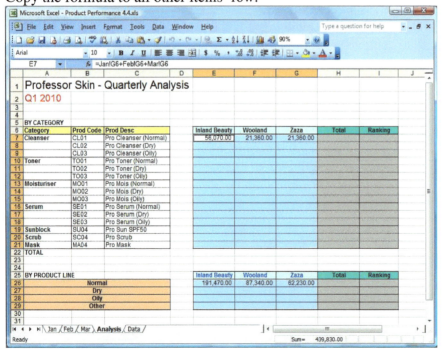

Step 5 – Evaluation

5.1 After complete copy all formula for each items' row, you can now sum up the total by each product and by each product line.

To ensure that you retrieve the data correctly, counter check by total up the sales revenue by customer at Line 30.

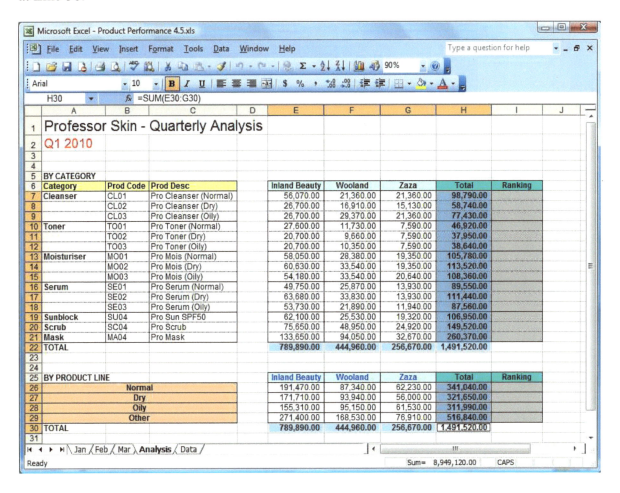

5.2 With all data ready on Report' sheet, we can start rank the product.

    5.21 Insert RANK formula. Click on cell I7. Type in as follow:
    =RANK(H7,$H$7:$H$9)

Arguments	Description
H7	The item to be rank in the list.
$H$7:$H$9	Is the list to be taken into the account of ranking.

Table 4.45

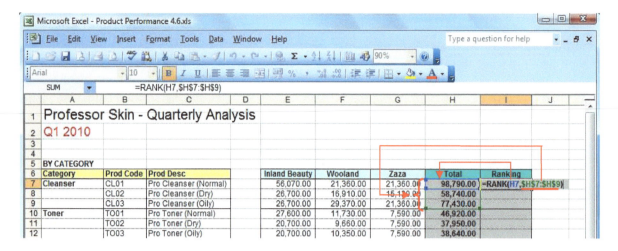

5.22 When the formula complete, press **ENTER** on the keyboard.

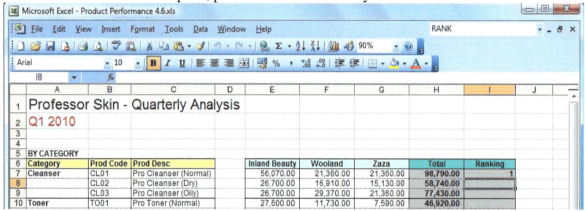

5.23 Repeat Step 5.21 – 5.22 on cell I8 & I9 with the following RANK arguments:

Cell	Formula
I8	=RANK(H8,$H$7:$H$9)
I9	=RANK(H9,$H$7:$H$9)

The difference of the formula argument is the Prod Code's cell to be ranked (font highlight in blue above) as explain earlier in Table 4.45.

Normal PL is the best seller among Cleanser Category.

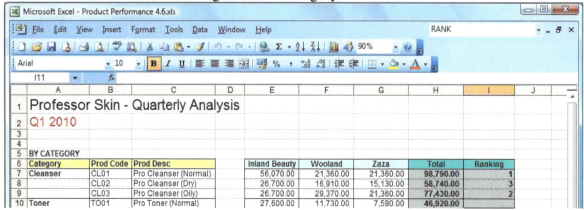

5.24 Repeat Step 5.21 by category for Toner, Moisturiser, Serum & Other Product with the following RANK arguments:

Category	Formula
Toner	
I10	=RANK(H10,$H$10:$H12)
I11	=RANK(H11,$H$10:$H12)
I12	=RANK(H12,$H$10:$H12)
Moisturiser	
I13	=RANK(H13,$H$13:$H15)
I14	=RANK(H14,$H$13:$H15)
I15	=RANK(H15,$H$13:$H15)
Serum	
I16	=RANK(H16,$H$16:$H18)
I17	=RANK(H17,$H$16:$H18)
I18	=RANK(H18,$H$16:$H18)
Other	
I19	=RANK(H19,$H$19:$H21)
I20	=RANK(H20,$H$19:$H21)
I21	=RANK(H21,$H$19:$H21)

The difference of the formula argument this time is the Prod Code's cell to be ranked AND also the Category's list to be taken into account of ranking (font highlight in blue above) as explain earlier in Table 4.45.

5.25 Repeat Step 5.21 By Product Line for Normal, Dry, Oily & Other with the following RANK arguments:

Product Line	Formula
Normal (I26)	=RANK(H26,$H$26:$H$29)
Dry (I27)	=RANK(H27,$H$26:$H$29)
Oily (I28)	=RANK(H28,$H$26:$H$29)
Other (I29)	=RANK(H29,$H$26:$H$29)

The difference of the formula argument this time is the Product Line's cell to be ranked AND also the Product Line's list to be taken into account of ranking (font highlight in blue above) as explain earlier in Table 4.45.

Now, ranking is completed. We can review that which product line is the best seller by Product Category and also which Product Line is the best seller for All Categories.

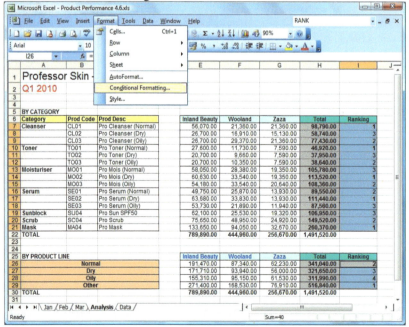

5.3 Lastly, to make the best seller eye catching, we can do conditional formatting.

    5.31 Select cell I7 - I21 & I26 - I29 > Go to Menu Bar > Click 'Format' > Click 'Conditional Formatting'.

5.32 'Conditional Formatting' window appeared.
   Click on 2nd drop down box > Select 'equal to'.

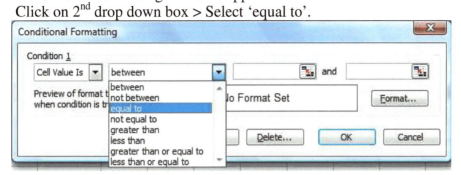

5.33 Type '1' in the text box & Click on 'Format' button.

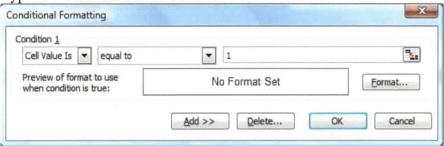

5.34 'Format Cells' window appeared.
   Click on 'Color' drop down box > Select 'Red' color > Click 'OK'.

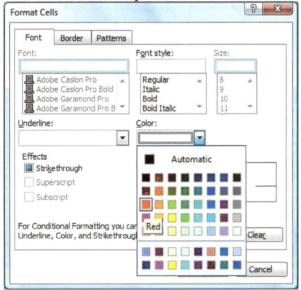

5.35 Back to 'Conditional Formatting' window. Click 'OK' again.
   Take notice that the preview has changed to the format you have selected.

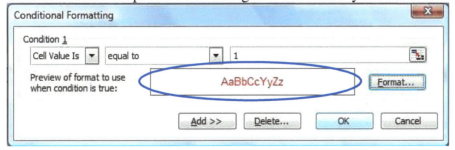

All the Number 1 Best Seller is displayed as RED. The Quarterly Analysis report has been fully completed for management to review.

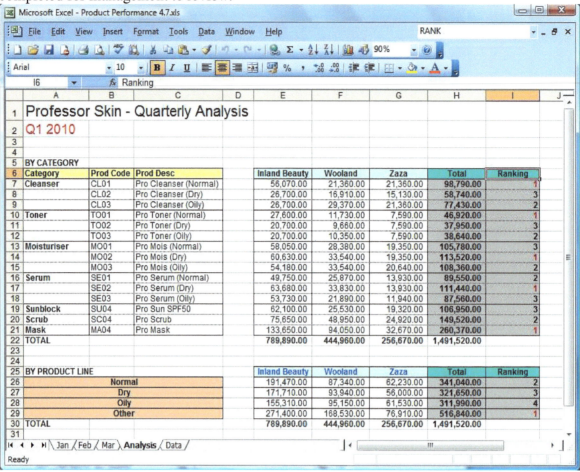

Step 6 – Save Automate Report

The Automate Report is now complete. You can now use this Automate Report to generate the report automatically for you in the next quarter and so on by just entering the data in the spreadsheet upon receive the hardcopy document of Invoice/DO.

You can see the benefits of storing the data in spreadsheet in database format instead of key-in the data straight away in the report format. With this data storing method, it is more flexible to utilize the data in different manner and can generate as many different requirement report as and when.

Note when storing data in the next month or next quarter:
- For storing next month data in the same quarter, key-in the data following the database format created the first time on the spreadsheet continue from the last row stored.
- For the next new quarter report, save it under a new file name.
  Eg: The Quarter 1 Automate Report save as 'Product Performance Analysis Q1.xls' and the next quarter as 'Product Performance Analysis Q2.xls' and so forth.
- For storing data in a new quarter report, delete all the data in spreadsheet while leaving the field name and start from Row 2 onwards.
- All these data can be copied out again to a new file under the same spreadsheet by end of the year to do other type of annual analysis as long as the database format is the same.

Storing next month data in the same quarter

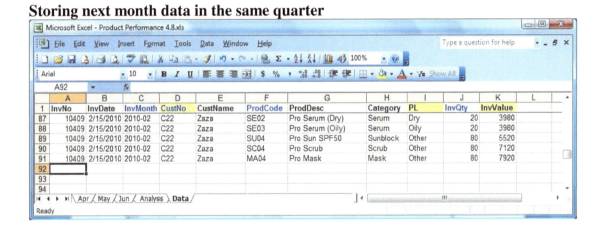

Storing data in a new quarter report

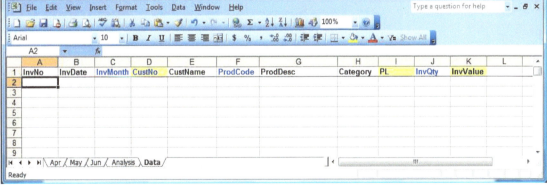

Okay after you have successfully completed this Scenario 4 Automate Report tutorial, you can try to adapt your own similar scenario in your company.

4.5 Scenario 5 : Program Milestone Report

Scenario Description

A product manager in a distributor company runs a program to boost sales for a particular product category for 1 month period. On top of the product promotion given to end user and dealers, the internal sales team will also be rewarded with incentive to make the program more successful. Target is set for every sales person in line with their region and they will be rewarded with incentive upon achieving their sales target.

The product manager has to prepare program milestone report on a weekly basis:
- to monitor the on-going result and take necessary action if required.
- to update the management on the on-going program result.

Step 1 – Create Report Template

1.1 Open a new excel file & create the report template in Sheet1 OR
Open the workbook 'Program Milestone 5.0.xls' to continue the tutorial.

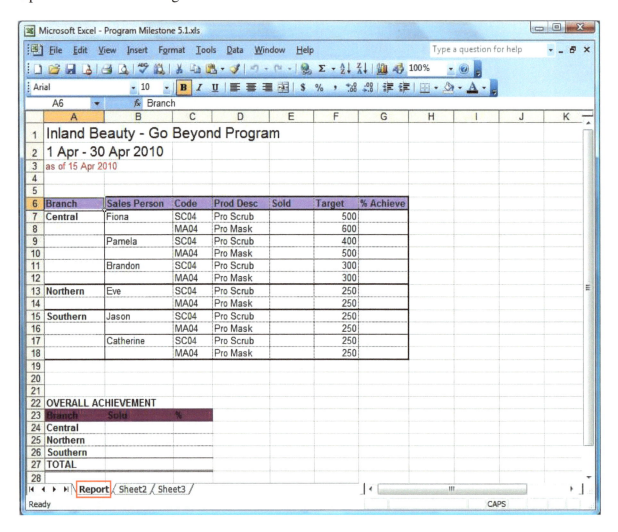

1.2 Rename Sheet1 as 'Report'.

Step 2 – Retrieve Data

2.1 Go to Sheet2 and place your cursor at cell A1 to begin import data / paste the data.
For this scenario, the filtering criteria would be Product Code for the brand and Date for the program running period.

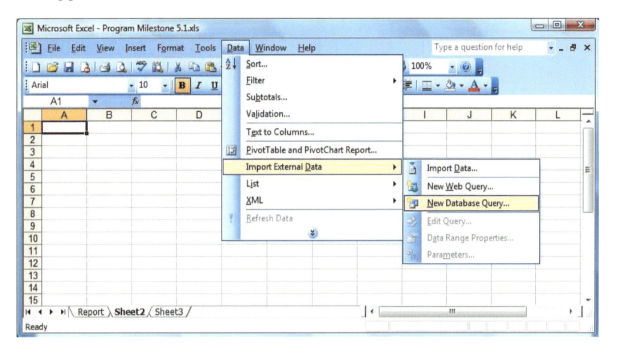

2.2 Rename Sheet2 as 'Data' when data import completed.

For tutorial & learning purpose, the workbook 'Stock Performance 2.0.xls' already contained the below data to simulate the data import completed.

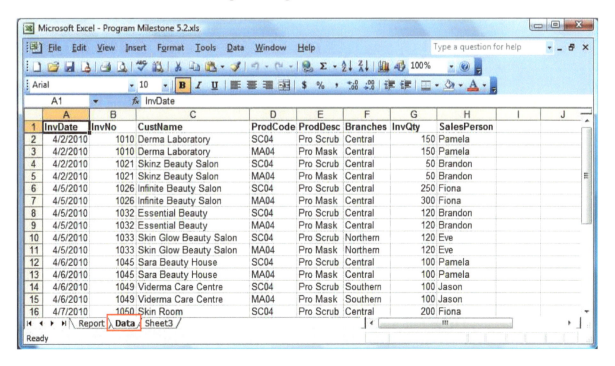

Step 3 – Insert Formula

3.1 Column G in 'Data' sheet is the data to be retrieved.
   While Columns D & H are the conditions to retrieve Column G.
   Change their font color to Blue to ease you later when inserting formula.

'Data' sheet

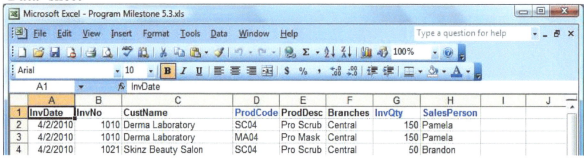

3.2 Go to 'Report' sheet.
   Column E in 'Report' sheet is the column to retrieve the data from 'Data' sheet.
   Change the font color to Blue as well for easy reference.

'Report' sheet

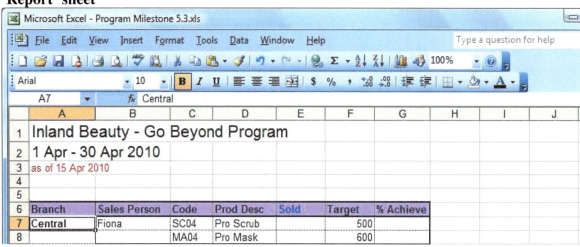

See below table for a better view.

'Report' sheet	**Retrieve from**	**'Data' sheet**
Column E – Sold	=	Column G – InvQty

Table 4.51

3.3 Insert SUM & IF formula.

   3.31 Click on cell E7. Type in as follow:
      =SUM(IF((Data!$H$1:$H$100=$B7)*(Data!$D$1:$D$100=$C7), Data!$G$1:$G$100))

Arguments	Description
Data!$H$1:$H$100=$B7	Search Column H in 'Data Sheet' from Row 1 to 100 where the items match B7 in 'Report Sheet'.
Data!$D$1:$D$100=$C7	Search Column D in 'Data Sheet' from Row 1 to 100 where the items match C7.
Data!$G$1:$G$100	Add the values in Column G from Row 1 to 100 for the rows that match the 2 conditions above.

Table 4.52

Note: As explained earlier in past scenario, I just specify the row up to 100 to make it simple for your learning. To be safe, you can specify the row up to 1,000 or even 10,000 depends on how large your data is as Excel can store up to 65,535 rows maximum.

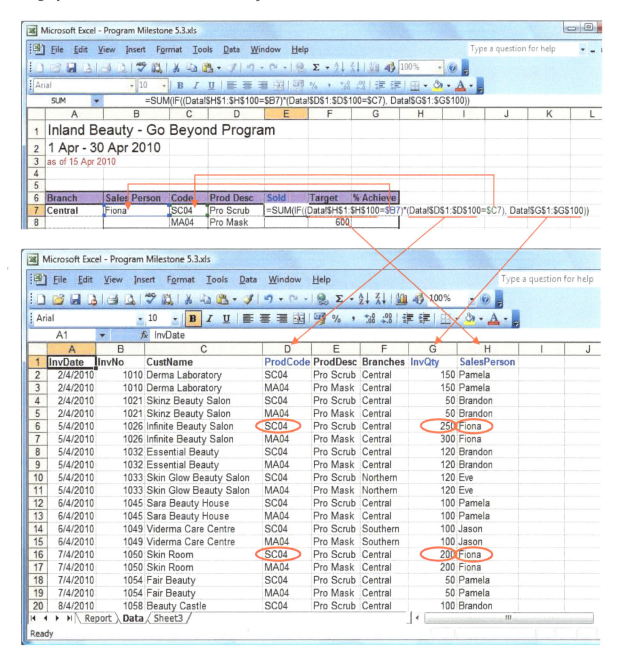

3.32 When the formula complete, press **ENTER** on the keyboard. Press **F2** on keyboard, and then press **CTRL+SHIFT+ENTER** to enter as array formula.

The data is successfully retrieved and shown in cell E7.

Important: The SUM & IF formulas combination must be entered as array formulas. If the formula is not entered as array formula, the error #VALUE! or 0 is returned. When in array formula [enclosed in braces { }], SUM & IF will return 0 too by default if there isn't any record found to be sum.

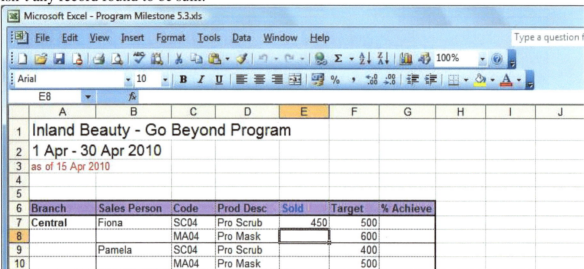

3.4 Insert Other Formula for the remaining columns.

Column	Description	Explanation
G	Formula: =E7/F7	To compute percentage achieve

Table 4.53

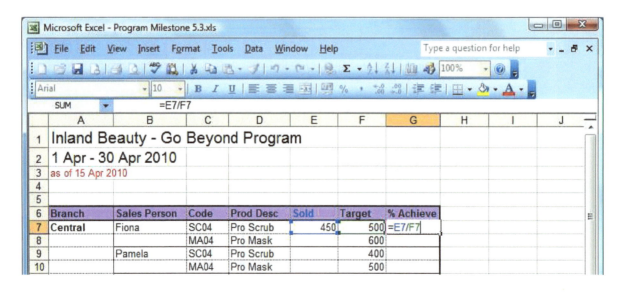

Step 4 – Copy Formula
Copy the formula to all other items' row.

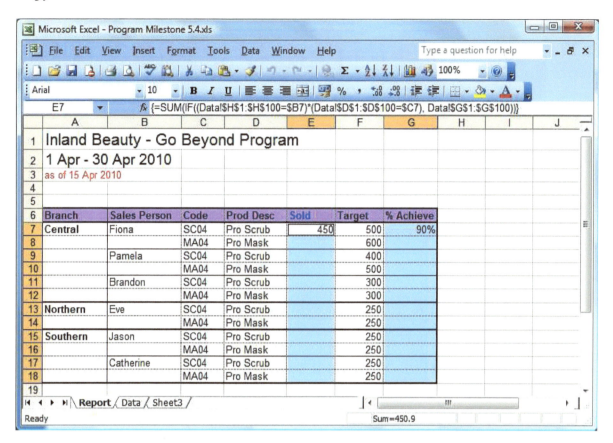

But take note that for cell E8, E10, E12, E14, E16 & E18, the 1st argument in the formula has to refer to the cell that contain the sales person name otherwise it is referring to the empty cell and can't retrieve any data unless you insert the sales person name in every cell in Column B.

Cell	Formula
E8	=SUM(IF((Data!$H$1:$H$100=$B7)*(Data!$D$1:$D$100=$C8), Data!$G$1:$G$100))
E10	=SUM(IF((Data!$H$1:$H$100=$B9)*(Data!$D$1:$D$100=$C8), Data!$G$1:$G$100))
E12	=SUM(IF((Data!$H$1:$H$100=$B12)*(Data!$D$1:$D$100=$C8), Data!$G$1:$G$100))
E14	=SUM(IF((Data!$H$1:$H$100=$B13)*(Data!$D$1:$D$100=$C8), Data!$G$1:$G$100))
E16	=SUM(IF((Data!$H$1:$H$100=$B15)*(Data!$D$1:$D$100=$C8), Data!$G$1:$G$100))
E18	=SUM(IF((Data!$H$1:$H$100=$B17)*(Data!$D$1:$D$100=$C8), Data!$G$1:$G$100))

Important:
Please take note of the cell addressing if you did not use or miss out the '$' in the data range to search in the formula when you copy the formula using fill handler / fill down.

Step 5 – Evaluation

5.1 With all data retrieved on 'Report' sheet, you can sum up the total for each branch.

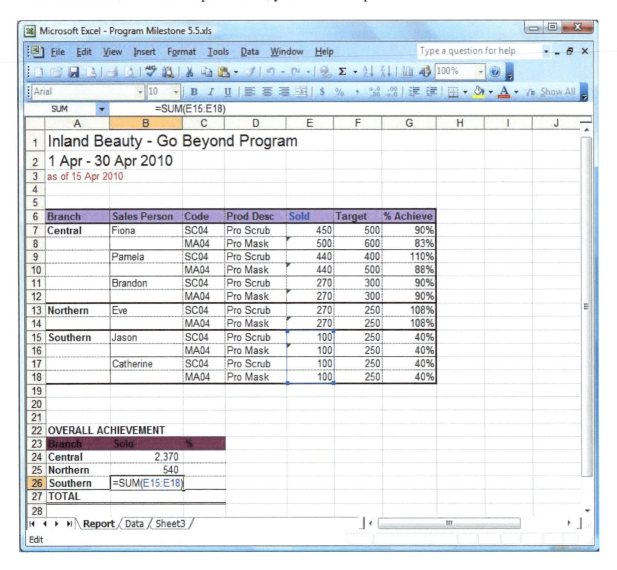

5.2 Lastly, compute the '%' to evaluate the overall achievement of branches.

Step 6 – Save Automate Report

The Automate Report is now complete. You can now use this Automate Report to generate the report automatically for you next time just with a few clicks.

Just import the updated data next time in 'Data' sheet, and wait for the data downloading complete. Then you can go to 'Report' sheet to view the program milestone report in the formatted way you want.

If you want the report to show revenue generated beside quantity sold, you can customized yourself by adding unit price & revenue column in the report.

Note when importing data next time:
- Place the cursor in cell A1.
- You may choose to delete or keep your previous data in Row 1 onwards because the data imported will replace the old data.
- Select the same database table & fields exactly in its order like the first time.
- If you would like to keep every updated report, then save a new file everytime. Eg: The first Automate Report as 'Prog Milestone Week1.xls' and the next update as 'Prog Milestone Week2.xls' and so forth.

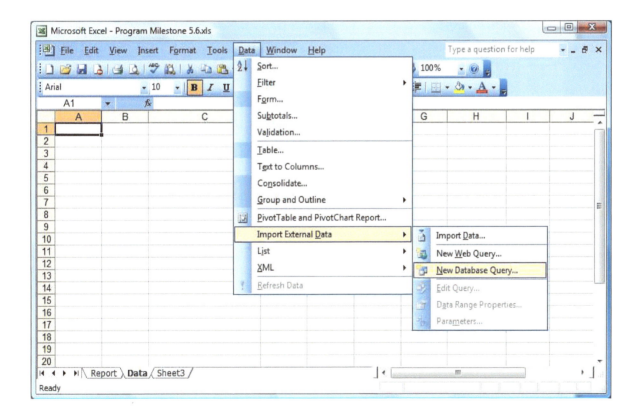

Okay after you have successfully completed this Scenario 5 Automate Report tutorial, you can try to adapt your own similar scenario in your company.

4.6 Scenario 6 : Program Status Report

Scenario Description

One of the Credit Card Marketing Department in a Bank runs a card members privilege program quarterly to encourage card spending by inviting merchants cover categories from Dining, Hotel & Travel, Beauty & Fitness and Shopping to offer special discounts & privileges to its card member.

The Privilege Program only limits to 20 merchants each quarter and require an average spread among the participating merchants.

The Senior Marketing Executive who takes lead of the program requires to report the program status weekly to the management with the following information:

- The number of Participating Merchants in total and by category from the Proposed Merchant Invitation List.
- The number of the Participating Merchants that are using their bank's card terminal (term as On-Us by the Bank Industry) as priority need to be given to On-Us Merchants.
- The number of Participating Merchants who have submitted the offers.

Step 1 – Create Report Template

1.1 Open a new excel file & create the report template in Sheet1 OR
Open the workbook 'Program Status 6.0.xls' to continue the tutorial.

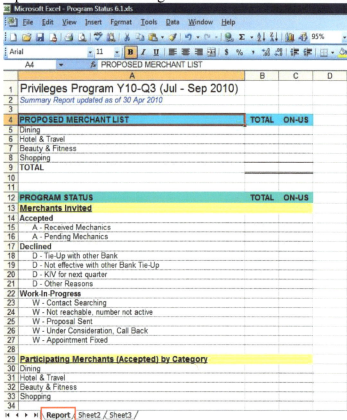

1.2 Rename Sheet1 as 'Report'.

Step 2 – Retrieve Data

2.1 For this scenario, information is not to be obtained from a system but obtain from the marketing executive themselves while dealing with the merchants. In this case, it is best to create a list and store the data in the list every time when there is an update/progress.

Go to 'Sheet2' and create the necessary field as follow:

1. No
2. Merchant
3. Category
4. On-Us
5. Contact Person
6. Designation
7. Tel No
8. Email
9. Status
10. Remark 1
11. Remark 2

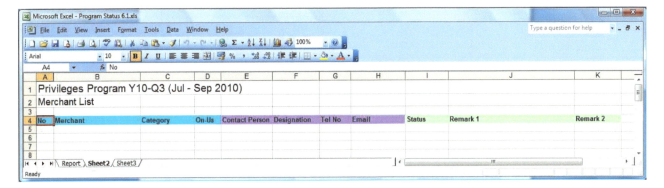

2.2 Now, the data field had been identified & created. The proposed merchant list needs to be entered by the marketing executive into the list.

For tutorial & learning purpose, the workbook 'Merchant List.xls' already contained the data to simulate the executive already entered all proposed merchant into the list.

Copy all the data from 'Sheet1' in 'Merchant List.xls' to 'Sheet2' in 'Program Status 1.0.xls' & rename it as 'Merchant List'.

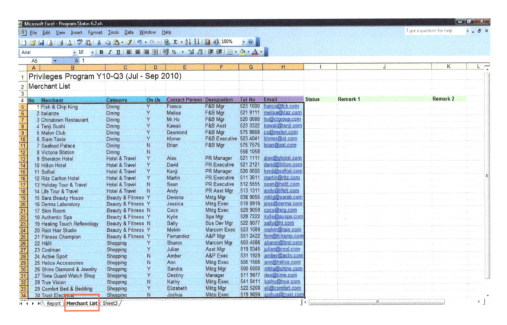

2.3 Create drop-down menu in the list.

As for Status & Remark 1 field will have the same data options determine by the program leader, it will be best to create a drop-down menu to ensure consistency of the data input.

2.31 Go to 'Sheet3' and type the following in Column A & B.
Rename 'Sheet3' to 'DropDown Menu'.

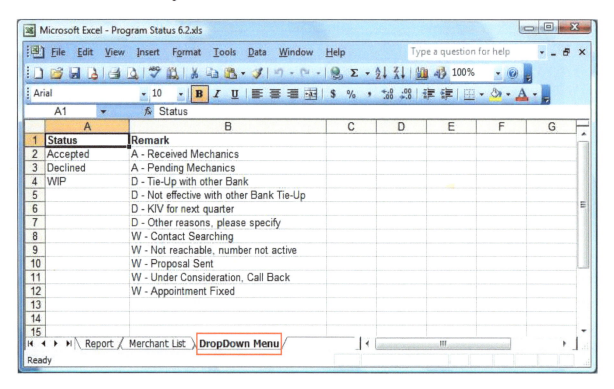

2.32 Select cell A2 to cell A4 > Click the 'Name Box' at the left end > Type 'Status' > press **ENTER** on keyboard.

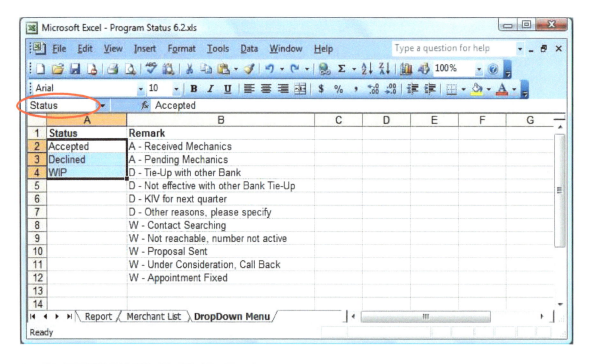

2.33   Select cell B2 to cell B12 > Click the 'Name Box' at the left end > Type 'Remark' > press **ENTER** on keyboard.

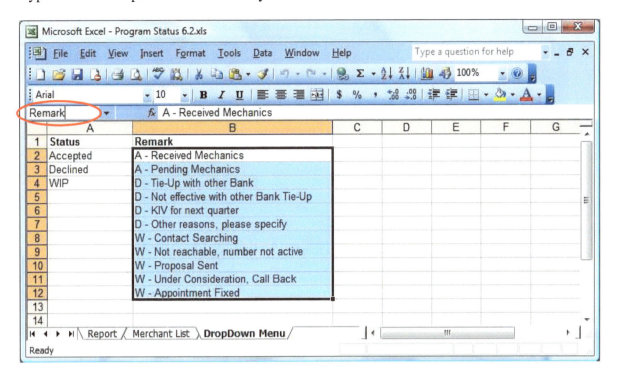

Note:
To ensure those names have been defined correctly, select cell A2 to cell A4 again / B2 to B12, and check whether the 'Name box' display 'Status' / 'Remark'. If 'Status' / 'Remark' is displayed on 'Name box', then the name is defined correctly, else redefined by repeat step 2.32 - 2.33.

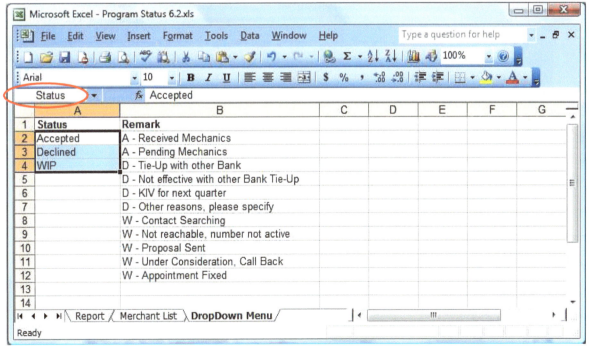

2.34 Select cell I5 to cell I50 > Click on Data Menu > Validation.

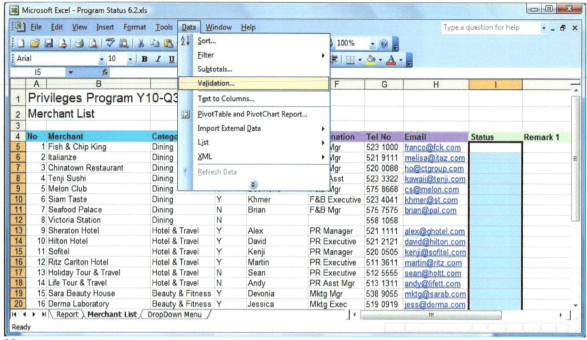

Note:

Cell is selected until I50 just in case the list get expanded, then the drop-down menu will still be available until I50. However, it can be added later on by repeating the same step if it is not set now.

2.35 'Data Validation' window appeared.

On the 'Settings' tab > 'Allow' drop-down > Select 'List'.

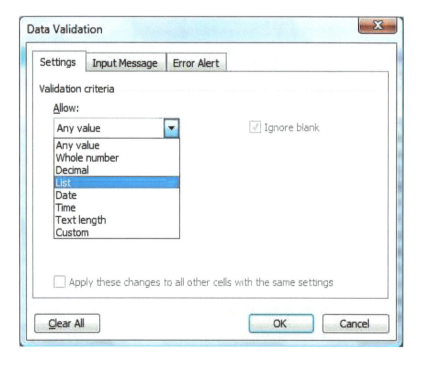

2.36 'Source' text box appeared.
Type '=Status' on the 'Source' text box > Click OK.

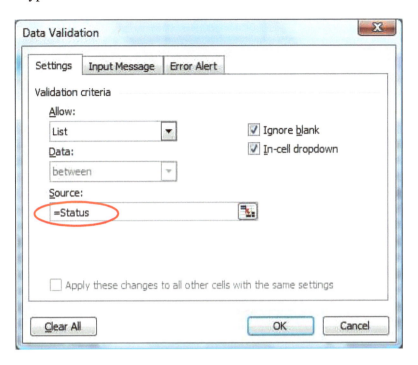

Important:

Ensure you include equal sign [=] in the 'Source' text box so that it can interpret that you are referring to the Status drop-down menu ('DropDown Menu'!$A$2:$A$4) you defined earlier.

Also make sure that the 'Ignore blank' & 'In-cell dropdown' checkbox is selected.

2.37 Select cell J5 to cell J50 > Click on Data Menu > Validation.

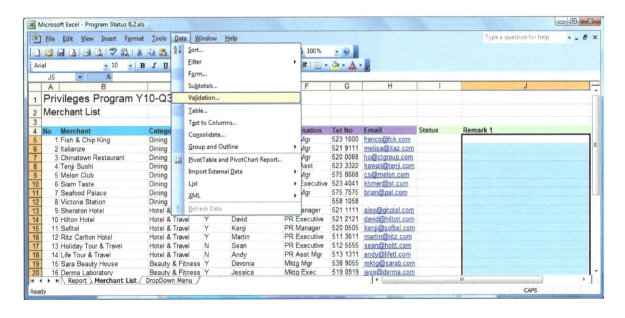

2.38 Repeat Step 2.35 - 2.36 with '=Remark' on the 'Source' text box this time.

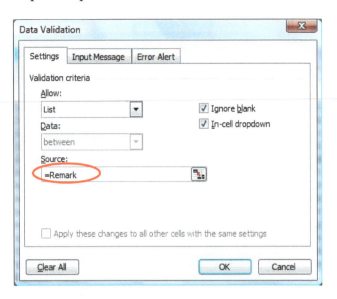

2.39 Go to 'Merchant List' sheet. Click on Column 'Status' drop-down. You can see the options defined earlier in 'DropDown Menu' sheet.

Same goes with Column 'Remark 1'. By creating drop-down menu, the executive can select from the drop-down when updating the status from time to time.

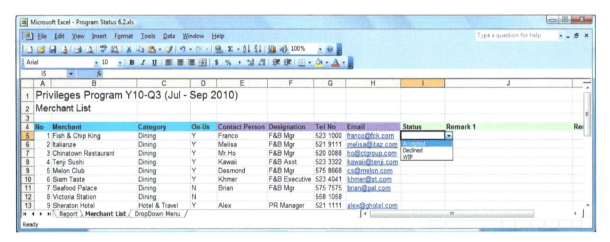

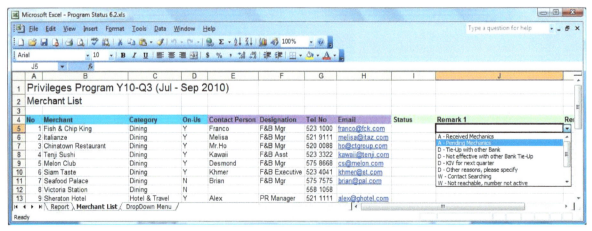

2.4 Assuming that the executive has updated the status for each merchant as of 30 Apr 2010.

For tutorial & learning purpose, the workbook 'Merchant List.xls' already contained the updated status. Go to 'Sheet2', copy the data from I5 - K34 to 'Merchant List' sheet in 'Prog Status 1.0.xls'.

'Remark 2' column is a free column to enter any text.

'Merchant List.xls' – Sheet2

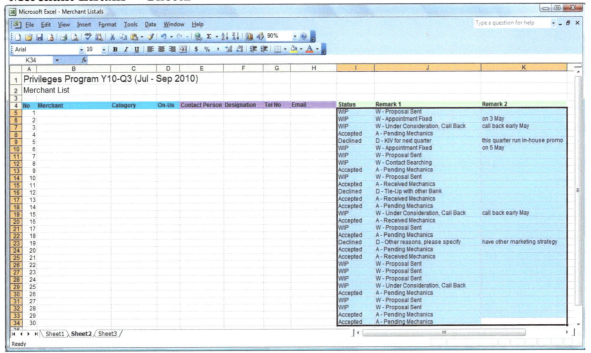

'Program Status 1.0.xls' – 'Merchant List' sheet

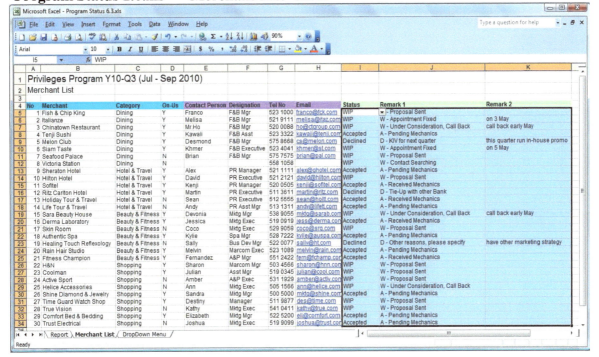

Step 3 – Insert Formula

3.1 Column C, D, I & J in 'Merchant List' sheet are the data to be counted.
Change their font color to Blue to ease you later when inserting formula.

'Merchant List' sheet

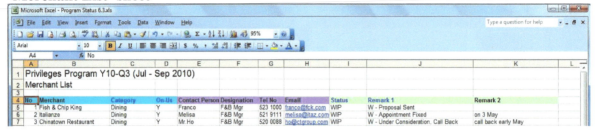

3.2 Go to 'Report' sheet.
Column B & C in 'Report' sheet are the column to count the data from 'Merchant List' sheet. Change the font color to Blue as well for easy reference.

'Report' sheet

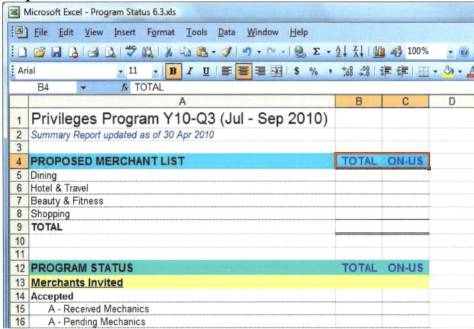

See below table for a better view.

'Report' sheet	Count from	'Merchant List' sheet
Column B – Total		
➢ Row 5-8	=	Column C – Category
➢ Row 15-33	=	Column J, C & I – Remark 1, Category & Status
Column C – On-Us		
➢ Row 5-8	=	Column C & D – Category & On-Us
➢ Row 15-33	=	Column C, D, I & J – as on above

Table 4.61

3.3 Insert COUNTIF formula.

3.31 Click on cell B5. Type in as follow:
=COUNTIF('Merchant List'!$C$5:$C$50, A5)

Arguments	Description
'Merchant List'!$C$5:$C$50	Count the occurrence in Column C from Row 5 to 50 in 'Merchant List' sheet.
A5	Count only if the values match A5 in 'Report' sheet.

Table 4.62

Note: As explained earlier in Step 2.34 scenario, I just specify the row up to 50 in case the list expands later. To be safe, you can specify the row up to 100 or even 150 depends on how far your list can expand.

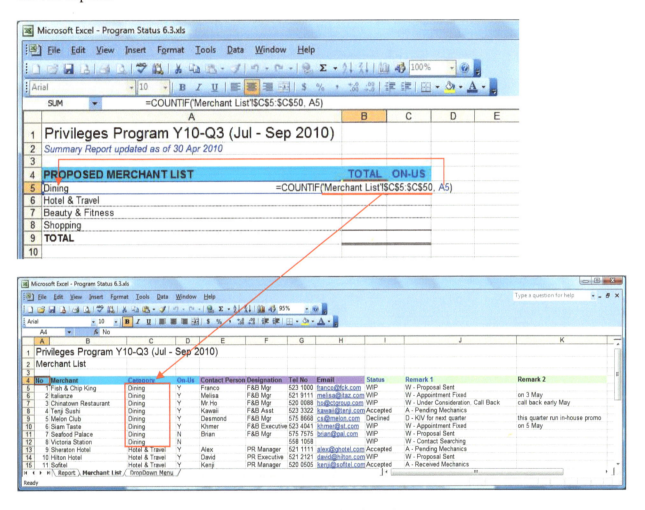

3.32 When the formula complete, press **ENTER** on the keyboard.
The data is successfully retrieved and shown in cell B5.

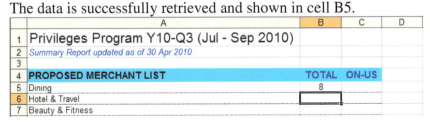

3.4 Insert COUNT & IF formula.

3.41 Click on cell C5. Type in as follow:
=COUNT(IF(('Merchant List'!$C$5:$C$50=A5)*('Merchant List'!$D$5:$D$34="Y"),))

Arguments	Description
'Merchant List'!$C$5:$C$50=A5	Count the occurrence in Column C from Row 5 to 50 in 'Merchant List' sheet where the values match A5 in 'Report' sheet.
'Merchant List'!$D$5:$D$34="Y"	Count the occurrence in Column D from Row 5 to 50 in 'Merchant List' sheet where the values match "Y" in 'Report' sheet.
3rd Argument : Blank [,]	In SUM & IF formula, the 3rd argument is to specify the range to be sum for values that match 1st & 2nd arguments. For COUNT & IF formula, it is not applicable as there is nothing to be sum. Therefore, just leave blank for 3rd argument. But make sure you specify the comma [,] or else the formula is incomplete.

Table 4.63

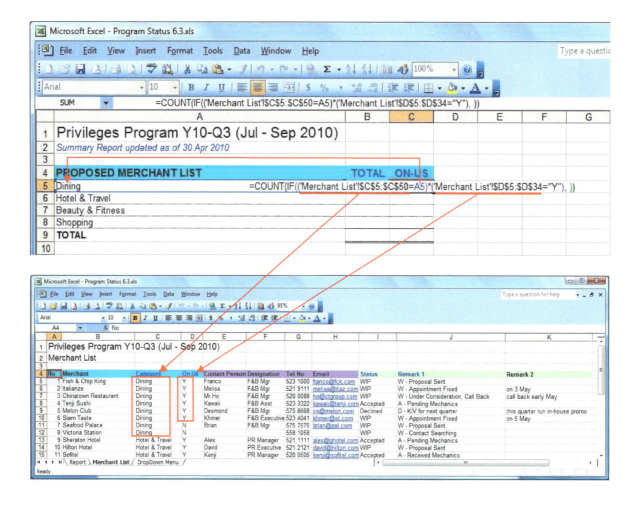

3.42 When the formula complete, press **ENTER** on the keyboard. Press **F2** on keyboard, and then press **CTRL+SHIFT+ENTER** to enter as array formula.

The data is successfully retrieved and shown in cell C5.

Important: The COUNT & IF formulas combination must be entered as array formulas. If the formula is not entered as array formula, the error value 1 is returned.

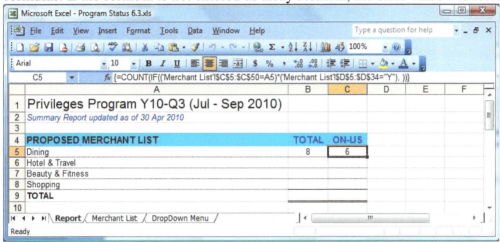

3.43 Repeat Step 3.41 - 3.42 on cell under 'Total' & 'On Us' with the following COUNT & IF arguments:

Cell	Formula
B15	=COUNTIF('Merchant List'!$J$5:$J$50, A15)
C15	=COUNT(IF(('Merchant List'!$J$5:$J$50=A15)*('Merchant List'!$D$5:$D$50="Y"),))
B30	=COUNT(IF(('Merchant List'!$C$5:$C$50=A30)*('Merchant List'!$I$5:$I$50="Accepted"),))
C30	=COUNT(IF(('Merchant List'!$C$5:$C$50=A30)*('Merchant List'!$I$5:$I$50="Accepted")*('Merchant List'!$D$5:$D$50="Y"),))

Note: Remember to enter as array formula for cell B30, C15 & C30.

The difference of the formula argument is the Column (font highlight in blue above) used to count the data from 'Merchant List' sheet as explain earlier in Table 4.61.

B15   Number of merchants that accepted to participate and have submitted the offers (promotion/offers mechanics).

C15   Number of merchants that accepted to participate and have submitted the offers and also On-Us merchants.

B30   Number of merchants that accepted to participate and under Dining category.

C30   Number of merchants that accepted to participate and under Dining category and also On-Us merchants.

Step 4 – Copy Formula

4.1 Copy cell B5 & C5 formula to row 6-8.

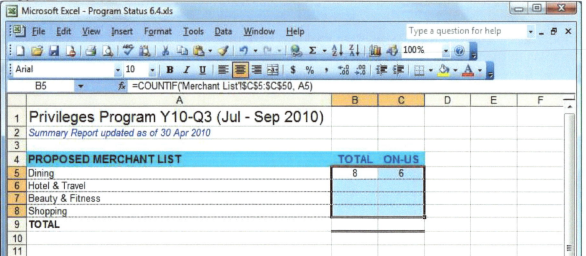

4.2 Copy cell B15 & C15 formula to row 16-27.

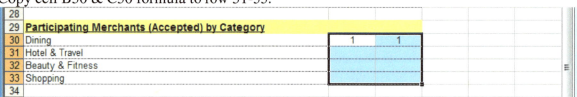

4.3 Copy cell B30 & C30 formula to row 31-33.

Important:

Please take note of the cell addressing if you did not use or miss out the '$' in the formula when you copy the formula using fill handler / fill down.

Also, the formula has to be copy separately as in Step 4.1 – 4.3 as the formula is different on the 3 sections in the report.

Step 5 – Evaluation

5.1 After complete copy all formula on the 3 sections in the report, you can now sum up the grand total at Row 9 & subtotal at row 14, 22 & 28.

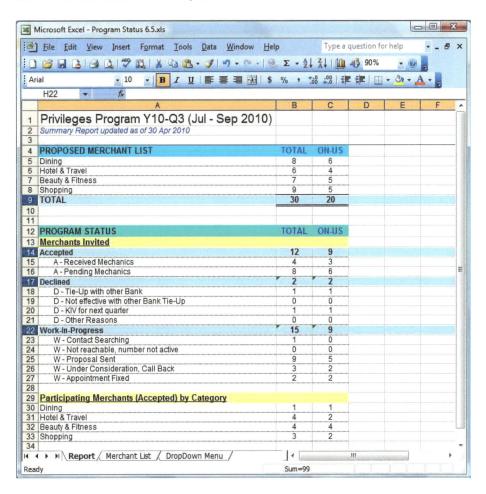

Note:

You can also use COUNTIF and COUNT & IF formula for the subtotal at row 14, 22 & 28. Column to be counted is I & J. None the less use SUM is easier.

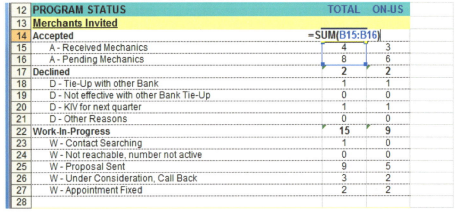

5.2 Now the program report is completed. It can be presented to the management to give a brief summary of the program status.

There are times that the management would like to know which merchants have participated. The merchant list can be presented to the management as well by 'Group' or 'Hide' the columns which are not important to the management.

'Group' column is a more user-friendly feature compares to 'Hide' column. Here, I will show you how.

5.21 Go to 'Merchant List' sheet, select Column E to H.

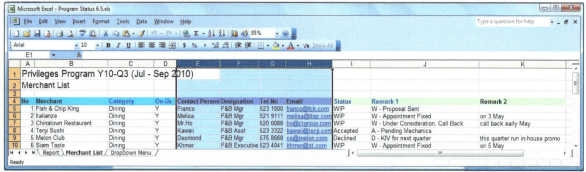

5.22 Go to Menu Bar > Click 'Data' > select 'Group and Outline' > click 'Group'.

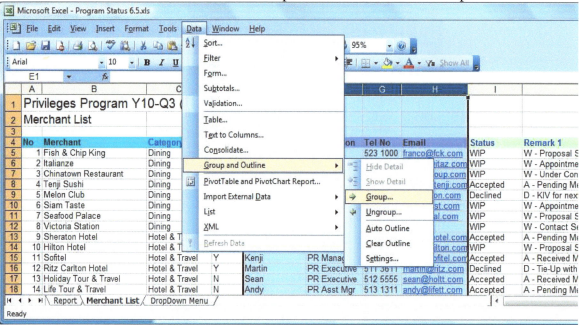

5.23 The 'Outline Symbol' appeared for the data/column you selected to group.

Click on the 'Outline Symbol' (minus sign) to hide the data.

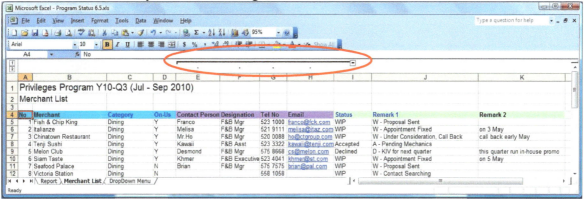

You can show or hide detailed data by clicking the plus sign, minus sign, and the numbers 1 or 2 indicating the outline level.

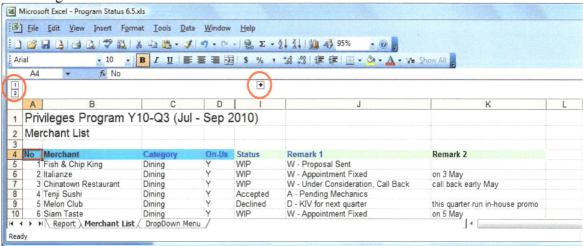

The merchants' contact is not important to the management (Column E to H).
Just click the minus sign to hide them when present the report & the list to management.

And the executive can click on the plus sign again when they work on the program.
It is more convenient and flexible compare to the usual hide/unhide column.

To ungroup the data anytime, go to Menu Bar > Click 'Data' > select 'Group and Outline' > click 'Ungroup'.

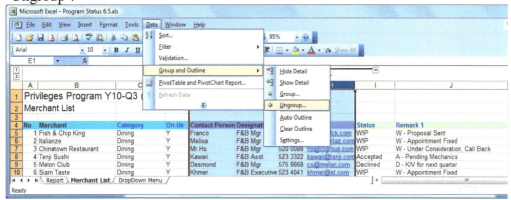

5.3 We can do conditional formatting in the list as well to further highlight merchants who have participated.

5.31 Select cell I5 – I50 > Go to Menu Bar > Click 'Format' > Click 'Conditional Formatting'.

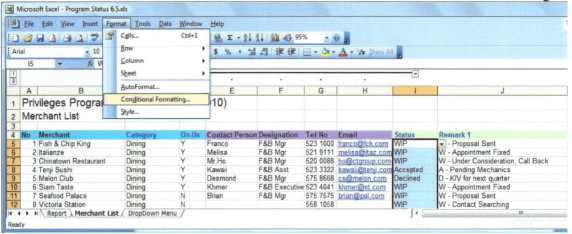

5.32 'Conditional Formatting' window appeared.
Click on 2nd drop down box > Select 'equal to'.

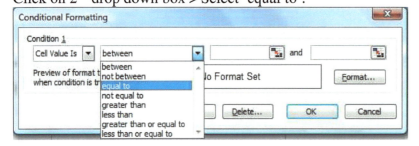

5.33 Type ="**Accepted**" in the text box & Click on 'Format' button.

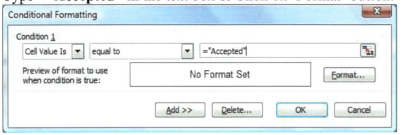

5.34 'Format Cells' window appeared.
Click on 'Color' drop down box > Select 'Blue' color > Click 'OK'.

5.35 Back to 'Conditional Formatting' window. Click 'OK' again.
Take notice that the preview has changed to the format you have selected.

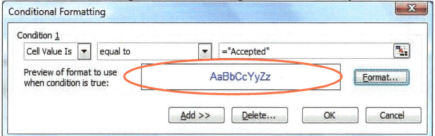

5.36 Repeat Step 5.21 – 5.35 on cell J5 – J50 with the following text:
To add 2nd condition, click on the 'Add' button at the bottom.

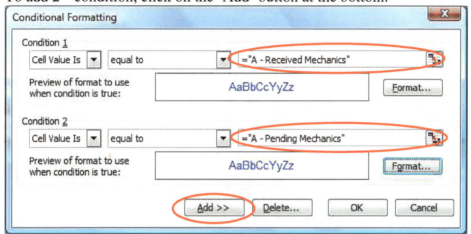

All the merchants that have accepted to participate is further highlighted in Blue.

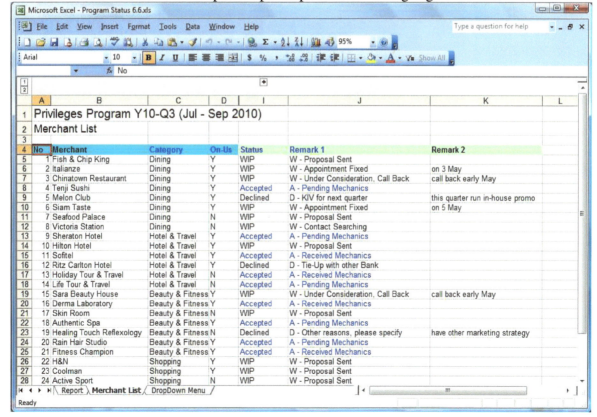

Step 6 – Save Automate Report

The Automate Report is now complete. You can now use this Automate Report to generate the report automatically for you from time to time whenever there is an update from the merchants or when the merchant list gets expanding.

Besides updating the status, you can store all merchants' information into the list and working along with it when need to contact or have discussion with the merchants. On top of that, it is also very flexible for you to group/hide those contacts information from management when it comes to reporting time.

Note when storing data from time to time or next quarter:

- For storing data in the same quarter, continue from the last row of merchant list. But please be reminded that the formula was set until Row 50. If the data extended beyond Row 50, then change the argument in the formula to Row 100 or more in order to have automated report. Explained under the note at Step 3.3.
- For the next quarter program report, save it under a new file name.
  Eg: The Quarter 3 Automate Report saves as 'Program Status Q3.xls' and the next quarter as 'Program Status Q4.xls' and so forth.
- For storing data in a new quarter report, delete all the data in spreadsheet while leaving the field name and start from the row after the field name.

Storing data in the same quarter report

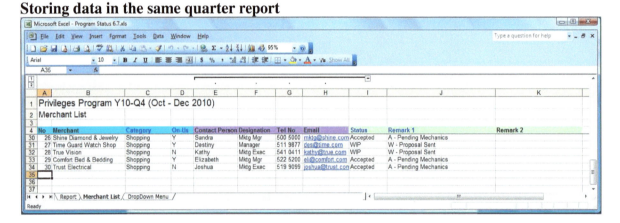

Storing data in a new quarter report

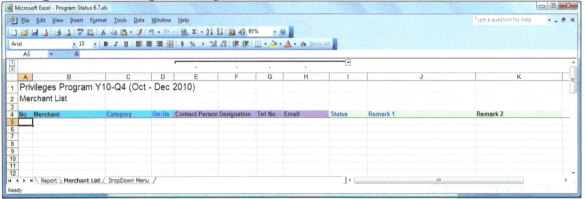

Okay after you have successfully completed this Scenario 6 Automate Report tutorial, you can try to adapt your own similar scenario in your company.

5.0 Useful Tips in Excel

In this chapter, you'll learn how to use a faster & easier way to achieve the same function when you work in Excel. Most of the tips are teaching you on how to use the keyboard shortcut key to speed up your work instead of moving your hand away from keyboard to mouse on & off to do your work.

5.1 Copy Formula (Fill down/Fill Right)

Open workbook 'Tips 5.1 - 5.4.xls' to continue the tutorial.

Usual Method:
Move the cursor to the corner of the cell > Drag the plus sign down / right using the mouse.
With this method, when you have a long list, it will over scroll when you drag using your mouse. This make you dizzy with the screen up & down. Sound familiar?

Tips :
Place cell pointer at cell F7 > Press & Hold the **SHIFT** key on keyboard > Press the arrow key ↓ on keyboard down until F14 > Press **CTRL + D** to fill down the formula.
Formula can be copied either down or right:

- Press ↓ & **CTRL + D** to fill down
- Press → & **CTRL + R** to fill right

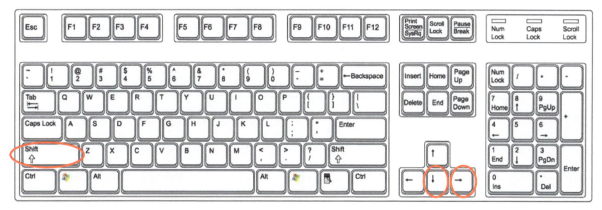

Note: Double check your formula after copy formula to avoid cell addressing changes if you did not use '$' in the formula.

5.2 Edit Formula [F2]

Usual Method:
Select the cell to edit > Move the mouse to the formula bar > Click on it to edit the cell on the formula bar

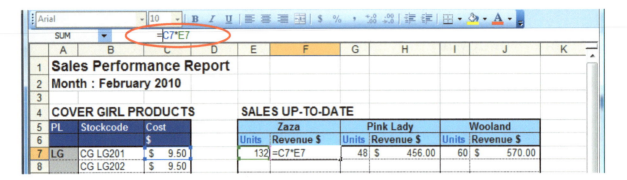

Tips :
Select the cell to edit > Press **F2** on keyboard > Edit from the cell itself

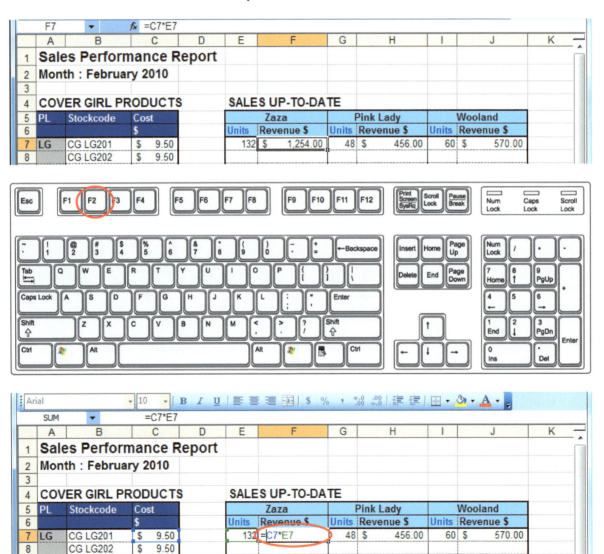

5.3 Fixed Cell Addressing [F4]

Usual Method:
Select the cell to edit > Press **F2** on keyboard > Move the cursor to the intended cell addressing > Press **$** sign on keyboard.

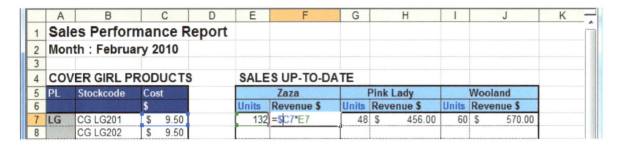

Tips :
Select the cell to edit > Press **F2** on keyboard > Move the cursor to the intended cell addressing > Press **F4** on keyboard.

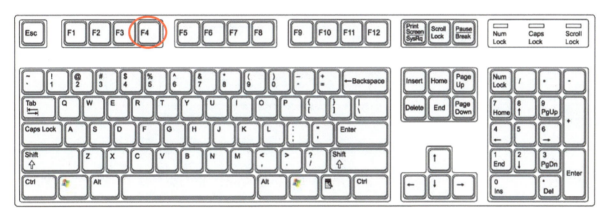

Press once – changes to $C$7 (<u>absolute</u> column and absolute row)

	COVER GIRL PRODUCTS				SALES UP-TO-DATE						
4	**COVER GIRL PRODUCTS**				**SALES UP-TO-DATE**						
5	**PL**	**Stockcode**	**Cost**			**Zaza**		**Pink Lady**		**Wooland**	
6			**$**		**Units**	**Revenue $**	**Units**	**Revenue $**	**Units**	**Revenue $**	
7	LG	CG LG201	$ 9.50		132	=$C$7*E7	48	$ 456.00	60	$ 570.00	
8		CG LG202	$ 9.50								

Press twice - changes to C$7 (relative column and absolute row)

	COVER GIRL PRODUCTS				SALES UP-TO-DATE						
4	**COVER GIRL PRODUCTS**				**SALES UP-TO-DATE**						
5	**PL**	**Stockcode**	**Cost**			**Zaza**		**Pink Lady**		**Wooland**	
6			**$**		**Units**	**Revenue $**	**Units**	**Revenue $**	**Units**	**Revenue $**	
7	LG	CG LG201	$ 9.50		132	=C$7*E7	48	$ 456.00	60	$ 570.00	
8		CG LG202	$ 9.50								

Press thrice - changes to $C7 (<u>absolute</u> column and relative row)

	COVER GIRL PRODUCTS				SALES UP-TO-DATE						
4	**COVER GIRL PRODUCTS**				**SALES UP-TO-DATE**						
5	**PL**	**Stockcode**	**Cost**			**Zaza**		**Pink Lady**		**Wooland**	
6			**$**		**Units**	**Revenue $**	**Units**	**Revenue $**	**Units**	**Revenue $**	
7	LG	CG LG201	$ 9.50		132	=$C7*E7	48	$ 456.00	60	$ 570.00	
8		CG LG202	$ 9.50								

5.4 Paste Special vs Copy Formula

Usual Method [for Copy Formula]:
Move the cursor to the corner of the cell > Drag the plus sign down / right using the mouse.
OR
Press & Hold **SHIFT** key on keyboard & then Press the arrow key ↓ / → on keyboard.

But for some cells' border that are formatted with different lines style, the lines style that you do not wish to copy, will be copied down as well. The Auto Fill options will appeared for you to select fill without formatting, if copy formula by drag the plus sign were used.

Tips :
Using Mouse:
1. Select the cell to copy formula > Right Click on mouse > Select 'Copy'.

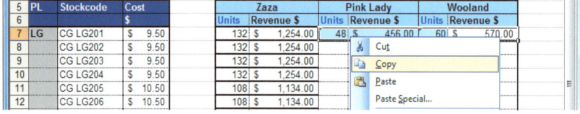

2. Select the cell to paste formula > Right Click on mouse > Select 'Paste Special'.

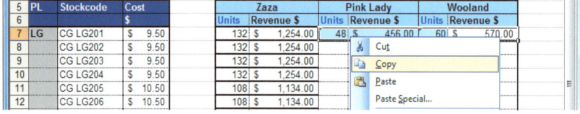

3. 'Paste Special' window appeared > Select 'Formulas' > Click 'OK'.

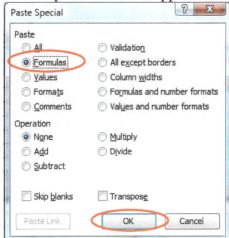

Using Keyboard:
1. Select the cell to copy formula > [Press **Right Click** on keyboard > Press **C** on keyboard] OR [Press **CTRL + C** on keyboard].
2. Select the cell to paste formula > Press **Right Click** on keyboard > Press **S** on keyboard.
3. 'Paste Special' window appeared > Press **F** on keyboard > Click 'OK'.

Note: You can identify the keyboard shortcut letter by the underline sign on the words.

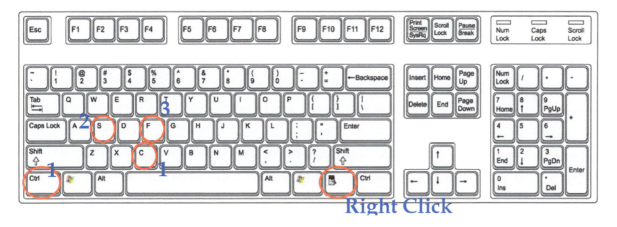

Paste Special vs Copy Formula

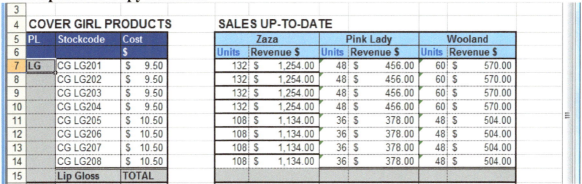

	COVER GIRL PRODUCTS		SALES UP-TO-DATE						
PL	Stockcode	Cost	Zaza		Pink Lady		Wooland		
		$	Units	Revenue $	Units	Revenue $	Units	Revenue $	
LG	CG LG201	$ 9.50	132	$ 1,254.00	48	$ 456.00	60	$ 570.00	
	CG LG202	$ 9.50	132	$ 1,254.00	48	$ 456.00	60	$ 570.00	
	CG LG203	$ 9.50	132	$ 1,254.00	48	$ 456.00	60	$ 570.00	
	CG LG204	$ 9.50	132	$ 1,254.00	48	$ 456.00	60	$ 570.00	
	CG LG205	$ 10.50	108	$ 1,134.00	36	$ 378.00	48	$ 504.00	
	CG LG206	$ 10.50	108	$ 1,134.00	36	$ 378.00	48	$ 504.00	
	CG LG207	$ 10.50	108	$ 1,134.00	36	$ 378.00	48	$ 504.00	
	CG LG208	$ 10.50	108	$ 1,134.00	36	$ 378.00	48	$ 504.00	
	Lip Gloss	TOTAL							

5.5 Find & Replace

Usual Method:
Go to 'Menu Bar' > Click 'Edit' > Click 'Find' > Choose 'Find' or 'Replace' features.

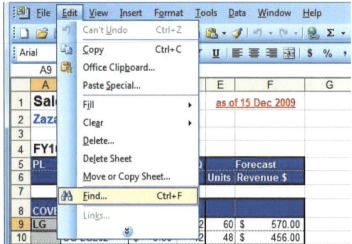

Tips :
Press **CTRL + F** on keyboard for Find / Press **CTRL + H** on keyboard for Replace.

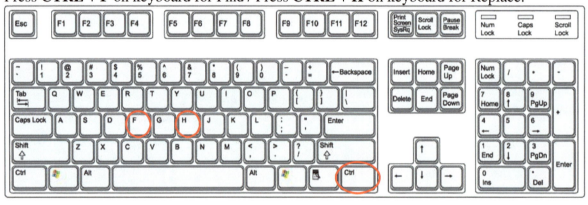

Besides, use the Find & Replace to replace words, it can be used to replace arguments in formula.

Open workbook 'Tips 5.5 - 5.8.xls' to continue the tutorial.

'Rpt PinkLady' sheet was copied from 'Rpt Zaza' sheet with all the formulas remained.
The difference of the formula between 'Rpt PinkLady' sheet and 'Rpt Zaza' sheet is the customer name which is "PinkLady" instead of "Zaza" for Column K, L, M & N.

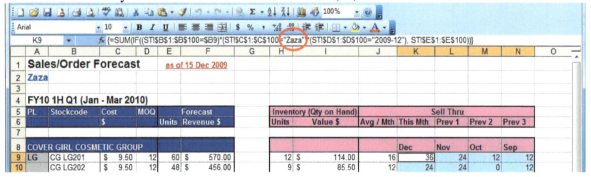

Refer to Chapter 4 - Scenario 3 under Step 5.3 – 5.8, the formula is re-inserted to the report all over again. Instead of delete the formula & re-insert all over again, we can use Find & Replace.

1. Place the cell selector at any cell (do not select multiple cells) to replace the entire sheet > Press **CTRL + H** on keyboard > 'Find and Replace' window appeared.
2. Type 'Zaza' in 'Find what' text box and 'Pink Lady' in 'Replace with' text box.
3. Click 'Replace All' button.

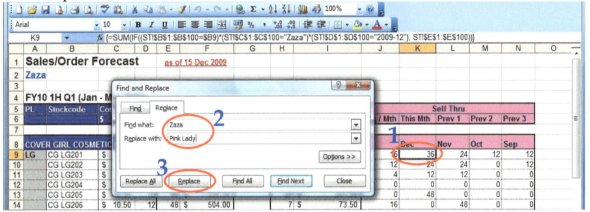

4. A message appeared inform you 69 replacements have been made > Click 'OK'.

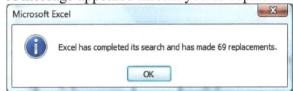

5. Close 'Find and Replace' window. The formula in Column K – N has been changed including the word in cell A2 has been changed from 'Zaza' to 'Pink Lady'.

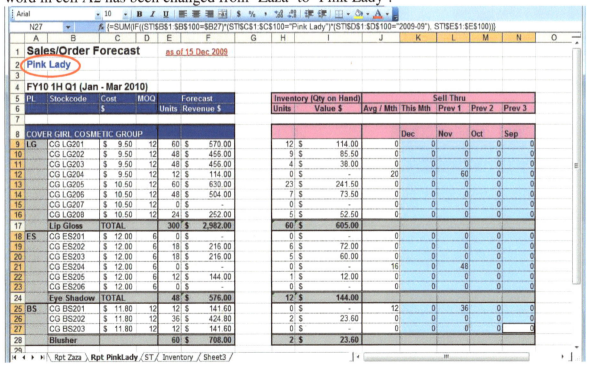

6. While for VLOOKUP formula in Column H, the difference of the formula between 'Rpt PinkLady' sheet and 'Rpt Zaza' sheet is the column number which is '3' instead of '2'.

But in Column H, there are other numbers '2' involved beside the '2' that we wish to change. They are cell H12, H20-H23 & H25-H27. Take note the '2' in the 1st argument of the formula. 'Find and Replace' will replace whatever number '2' in the cells.

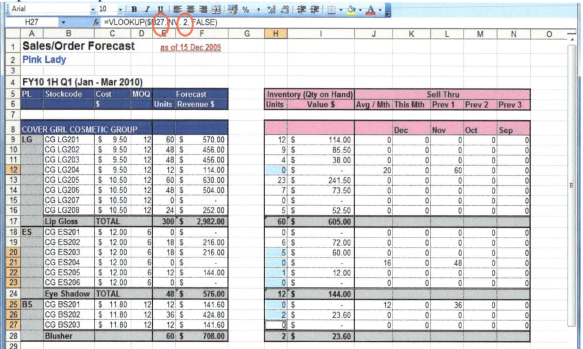

7. Therefore, select cell H9-H11, H13-16 & H18-H19 to replace selected cells only instead of entire sheet > Press **CTRL + H** on keyboard > 'Find and Replace' window appeared.
8. Type '2' in 'Find what' text box and '3' in 'Replace with' text box.
9. Click 'Replace All' button.

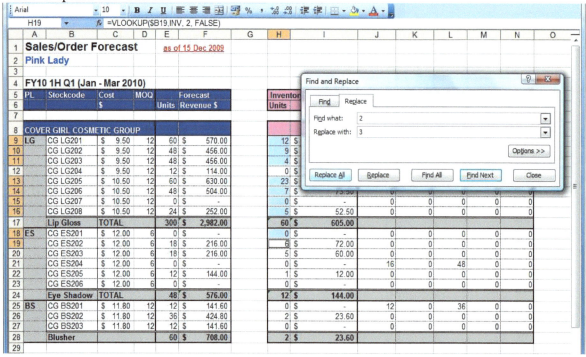

10. A message appeared inform you 9 replacements have been made > Click 'OK'.

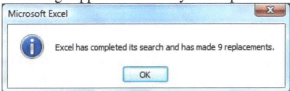

11. Close 'Find and Replace' window. The formula in selected cells has been changed.

| H19 | =VLOOKUP($B19,INV, 3, FALSE) |

	A	B	C	D	E	F	G	H	I	J	K	L	M	N	O
1	**Sales/Order Forecast**				*as of 15 Dec 2009*										
2	**Pink Lady**														
3															
4	**FY10 1H Q1 (Jan - Mar 2010)**														
5	PL	Stockcode	Cost	MOQ	Forecast			Inventory (Qty on Hand)		Sell Thru					
6			$		Units	Revenue $		Units	Value $	Avg / Mth	This Mth	Prev 1	Prev 2	Prev 3	
7															
8	**COVER GIRL COSMETIC GROUP**										Dec	Nov	Oct	Sep	
9	LG	CG LG201	$ 9.50	12	60	$ 570.00		0	$ -	0	0	0	0	0	
10		CG LG202	$ 9.50	12	48	$ 456.00		0	$ -	0	0	0	0	0	
11		CG LG203	$ 9.50	12	48	$ 456.00		0	$ -	0	0	0	0	0	
12		CG LG204	$ 9.50	12	12	$ 114.00		0	$ -	20	0	60	0	0	
13		CG LG205	$ 10.50	12	60	$ 630.00		0	$ -	0	0	0	0	0	
14		CG LG206	$ 10.50	12	48	$ 504.00		0	$ -	0	0	0	0	0	
15		CG LG207	$ 10.50	12	0	$ -		0	$ -	0	0	0	0	0	
16		CG LG208	$ 10.50	12	24	$ 252.00		0	$ -	0	0	0	0	0	
17		**Lip Gloss**	TOTAL		300	$ 2,982.00		0	$ -						
18	ES	CG ES201	$ 12.00	6	0	$ -		0	$ -	0	0	0	0	0	
19		CG ES202	$ 12.00	6	18	$ 216.00		0	$ -	0	0	0	0	0	
20		CG ES203	$ 12.00	6	18	$ 216.00		5	$ 60.00	0	0	0	0	0	
21		CG ES204	$ 12.00	6	0	$ -		0	$ -	16	0	48	0	0	
22		CG ES205	$ 12.00	6	12	$ 144.00		1	$ 12.00	0	0	0	0	0	
23		CG ES206	$ 12.00	6	0	$ -		0	$ -	0	0	0	0	0	
24		**Eye Shadow**	TOTAL		48	$ 576.00		6	$ 72.00						
25	BS	CG BS201	$ 11.80	12	12	$ 141.60		0	$ -	12	0	36	0	0	
26		CG BS202	$ 11.80	12	36	$ 424.80		2	$ 23.60	0	0	0	0	0	
27		CG BS203	$ 11.80	12	12	$ 141.60		0	$ -	0	0	0	0	0	
28		**Blusher**			60	$ 708.00		2	$ 23.60						
29															

12. For the remaining cell H12, H20-H23 & H25-H27, change the formula by editing formula on the cell OR copy formula from the replaced cell.

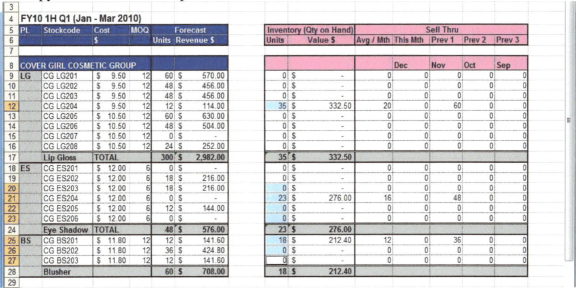

	A	B	C	D	E	F	G	H	I	J	K	L	M	N
3														
4	**FY10 1H Q1 (Jan - Mar 2010)**													
5	PL	Stockcode	Cost	MOQ	Forecast			Inventory (Qty on Hand)		Sell Thru				
6			$		Units	Revenue $		Units	Value $	Avg / Mth	This Mth	Prev 1	Prev 2	Prev 3
7														
8	**COVER GIRL COSMETIC GROUP**										Dec	Nov	Oct	Sep
9	LG	CG LG201	$ 9.50	12	60	$ 570.00		0	$ -	0	0	0	0	0
10		CG LG202	$ 9.50	12	48	$ 456.00		0	$ -	0	0	0	0	0
11		CG LG203	$ 9.50	12	48	$ 456.00		0	$ -	0	0	0	0	0
12		CG LG204	$ 9.50	12	12	$ 114.00		35	$ 332.50	20	0	60	0	0
13		CG LG205	$ 10.50	12	60	$ 630.00		0	$ -	0	0	0	0	0
14		CG LG206	$ 10.50	12	48	$ 504.00		0	$ -	0	0	0	0	0
15		CG LG207	$ 10.50	12	0	$ -		0	$ -	0	0	0	0	0
16		CG LG208	$ 10.50	12	24	$ 252.00		0	$ -	0	0	0	0	0
17		**Lip Gloss**	TOTAL		300	$ 2,982.00		35	$ 332.50					
18	ES	CG ES201	$ 12.00	6	0	$ -		0	$ -	0	0	0	0	0
19		CG ES202	$ 12.00	6	18	$ 216.00		0	$ -	0	0	0	0	0
20		CG ES203	$ 12.00	6	18	$ 216.00		0	$ -	0	0	0	0	0
21		CG ES204	$ 12.00	6	0	$ -		23	$ 276.00	16	0	48	0	0
22		CG ES205	$ 12.00	6	12	$ 144.00		0	$ -	0	0	0	0	0
23		CG ES206	$ 12.00	6	0	$ -		0	$ -	0	0	0	0	0
24		**Eye Shadow**	TOTAL		48	$ 576.00		23	$ 276.00					
25	BS	CG BS201	$ 11.80	12	12	$ 141.60		18	$ 212.40	12	0	36	0	0
26		CG BS202	$ 11.80	12	36	$ 424.80		0	$ -	0	0	0	0	0
27		CG BS203	$ 11.80	12	12	$ 141.60		0	$ -	0	0	0	0	0
28		**Blusher**			60	$ 708.00		18	$ 212.40					
29														

5.6 Sum multiple figures concurrently (at the same time)

Usual Method [to sum each column from Column J to N]:

Place cell pointer at J17 > Go to Toolbar > Click 'AutoSum' button > Press **ENTER** on keyboard > Repeat the whole process for each columns' cell at K17, L17, M17 & N17 one by one.

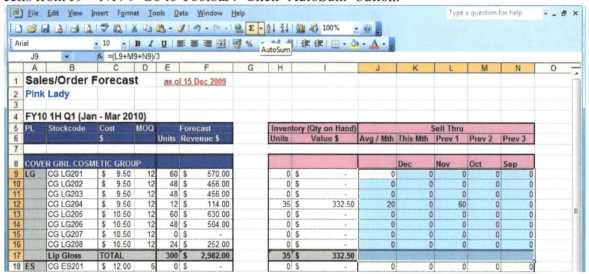

Tips :

Place the cell pointer at J9 > Press & Hold **SHIFT** key on keyboard > Click on N17 to select multiple cells from J9 – N17 > Go to Toolbar > Click 'AutoSum' button.

Multiple figures is sum up concurrently (at the same time) right after clicked.

5.7 Formatting multiple sheet concurrently (at the same time)

Usual Method [to edit the updated date to '21 Dec' in cell E1 for all report]:
Go to report sheet one by one > edit cell E1 with the same input every time.

	A	B	C	D	E	F	G	H	I	J	K	L	M	N	O
1	**Sales/Order Forecast**				*as of 21 Dec 2009*										
2	Zaza														
3															
4	FY10 1H Q1 (Jan - Mar 2010)														
5	PL	Stockcode	Cost	MOQ	Forecast			Inventory (Qty on Hand)		Sell Thru					
6			$		Units	Revenue $		Units	Value $	Avg / Mth	This Mth	Prev 1	Prev 2	Prev 3	
7															
8	COVER GIRL COSMETIC GROUP										Dec	Nov	Oct	Sep	
9	LG	CG LG201	$ 9.50	12	60	$ 570.00		12	$ 114.00	16	36	24	12	12	
10		CG LG202	$ 9.50	12	48	$ 456.00		9	$ 85.50	12	24	24	0	12	
11		CG LG203	$ 9.50	12	48	$ 456.00		4	$ 38.00	4	12	12	0	0	

Tips :

1. Select 'Rpt Zaza' sheet > Press & Hold **CTRL** key on keyboard > Click on 'Rpt Wooland' to select sheet one by one.
   OR
   Select 'Rpt Zaza' sheet > Press & Hold **SHIFT** key on keyboard > Click on 'Rpt Wooland' to select all sheets at once.

Note:
The sheet changed to white color when the sheets have been grouped together. You can also double confirm by checking on the title bar, the word **[Group]** is shown.

In Group mode, the active sheet is in **bold** like '**Rpt Zaza**'. If you click 'Rpt Wooland', it will become the active sheet and will change to **bold**.

Using CTRL key (select sheet one by one)

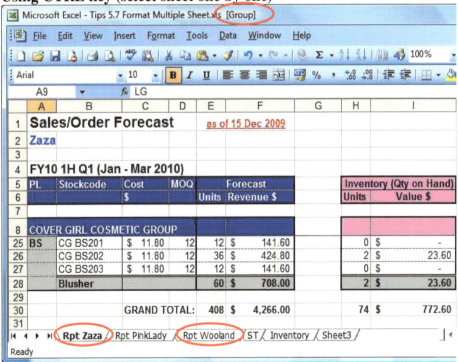

Using SHIFT key (select all sheets at once)

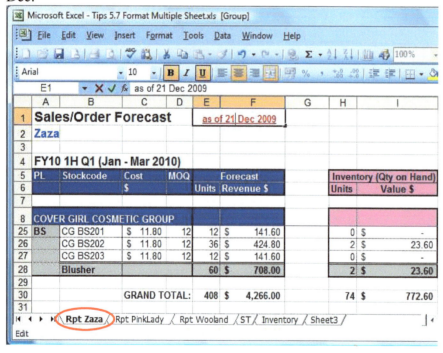

2. Place cell pointer at E1 on the active sheet 'Rpt Zaza' > Press **F2** on keyboard > edit the date to 21 Dec.

The date is changed to 'as of 21 Dec 2009' as well in the sheets that you have group earlier. Check it out in 'Rpt PinkLady' and 'Rpt Wooland' sheet.

You can perform any formatting like changing color, font size etc on the group mode and it will be reflected in the group of selected sheets. You can also move to any sheet to do the formatting, not necessary the first sheet 'Rpt Zaza'. The sheet you select to do the formatting is the active sheet which is in **bold**.

3. Besides formatting, you can insert formula in the group mode too if the group of sheets happen to have the same formula in the same cell address.

Ensure that the report sheets are still in group mode or else re-group > In active sheet 'Rpt Zaza' > Select cell J25 – N 28 > Go to Toolbar > Click 'AutoSum' button.

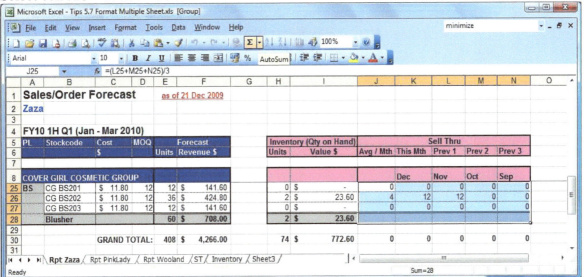

The formula is inserted in 'Rpt PinkLady' and 'Rpt Wooland' sheet too.

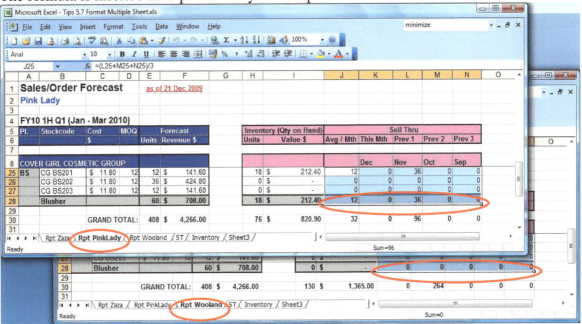

4. To ungroup / deselect all sheets > Click any sheet that is not selected (eg: 'ST' sheet) > all report sheets change back to grey color and **[Group]** word disappeared from title bar.
   OR
   Right Click at any sheet > menu appeared > choose 'Ungroup sheets > all report sheets change back to grey color and **[Group]** word disappeared from title bar.

5.8 Define Name

To remove Defined Name
In previous tutorial, I have taught on how to Define Name but not on how to remove them yet. Let's try to remove them now before move to the tip on the faster way to Define Name.

1. Go to 'Inventory' sheet > Click Insert Menu > Name > Define.

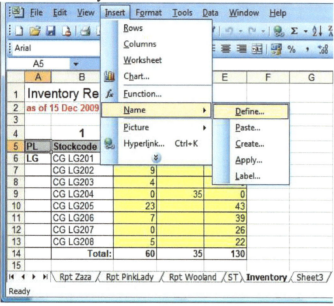

2. 'Define Name' window appeared.
    Select 'INV' in the list box > Click 'Delete' > 'INV' name disappeared > Click 'OK'.

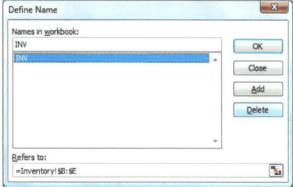

Go to report sheets and check inventory column H, the data become invalid as the VLOOKUP in column H uses 'INV' table array to refer to 'Inventory' sheet. (You can recall from Chapter 4 - Scenario 3 under Step 3.15).

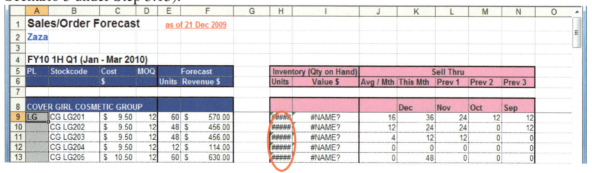

Usual Method [To Define Name]:

1. In 'Inventory' sheet > Select Column B, C, D & E > Click Insert Menu > Name > Define.

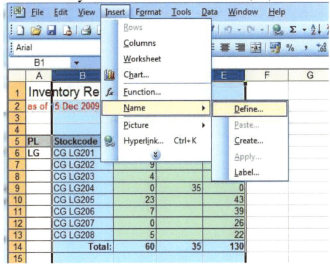

2. 'Define Name' window appeared.
    Type 'INV' on the 'Names in workbook' textbox > Click OK.

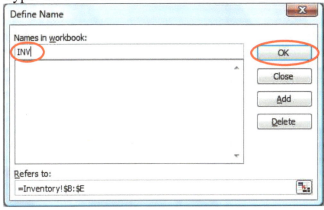

Tips :

1. In 'Inventory' sheet > Select Column B, C, D & E > Click the 'Name Box' at the left end > Type 'INV' > Press **ENTER** on keyboard.
    The name has been defined.

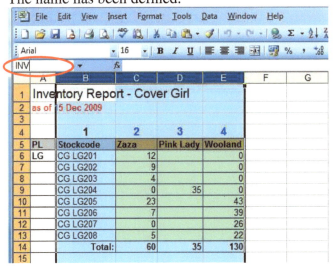

2. To ensure the 'INV' name has been defined, select Column B, C, D & E again and check whether the 'Name Box' displays 'INV'. If 'INV' is displayed on 'Name box', then the name is defined correctly, else redefined by repeat the same step above.

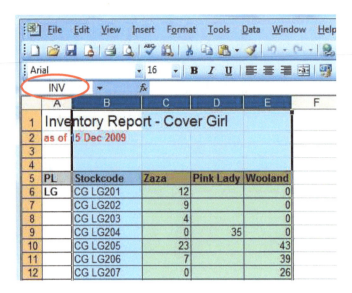

Go to report sheets again and check inventory column H, the data is valid again as the VLOOKUP in column H can identify the 'INV' table array name to refer to where to retrieve the data in 'Inventory' sheet .

5.9 Numbering

Open workbook 'Tips 5.9 - 5.10.xls' to continue the tutorial.

Usual Method:
In a list where you have to numbering the list, most will just type 1, 2, 3 and followed by the numbers subsequently one by one. If a list is a very long list, it is time consuming to key in the numbers one after another.

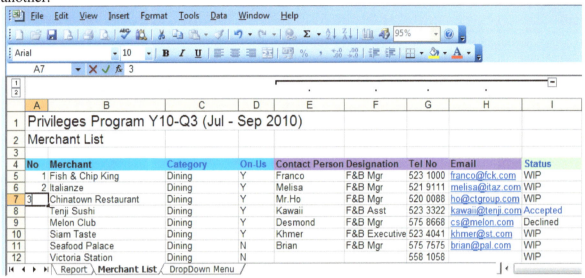

Tips :
1. Type '1' in cell A5 > Place cell pointer at cell A6 > Insert formula '=A5+1' > Press **ENTER** on keyboard.

2. Place cell pointer at cell A6 again > Press & Hold **SHIFT** key on keyboard > Press arrow key ↓ on keyboard down until cell A34 > Press **CTRL + D** on keyboard to number the entire list.

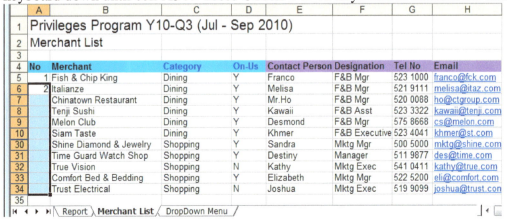

5.10 AutoFilter shortcut key at toolbar
*Applies to Microsoft Excel 2000 & 2003 only. Microsoft 2007 has added these buttons to Quick Access Toolbar.

Usual Method:

1. Sometimes, you only want the list to show specified record and filter out those unwanted.
   Place the cell pointer at any cell within the list > Click Data menu > Filter > AutoFilter.

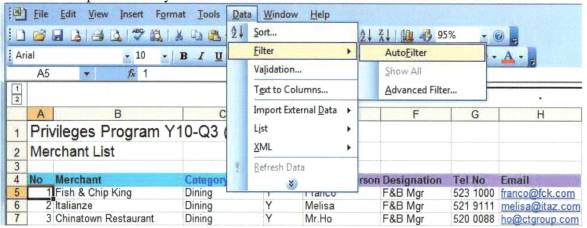

2. To show only merchants that still in WIP (Work-In-Progress), click at the 'Status' field drop-down list
   > Select 'WIP'.

3. The list shows merchants with 'WIP' status only.
   To further filter merchants under 'WIP' status that have 'Appointment Fixed' > Click at the 'Remark
   1' field drop-down list > Select 'W – Appointment Fixed'.

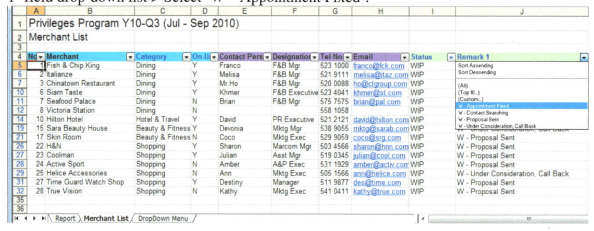

4. The list shows merchants with 'WIP' status and with 'W – Appointment Fixed' only.

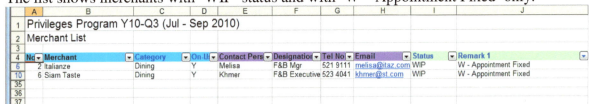

5. To view all data again > Click at the 'Remark 1' field drop-down list > Select (All).

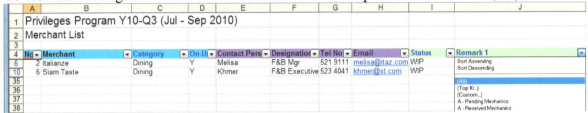

6. To remove the filter > Click 'Data' menu again > 'Filter' > Deselect the ' ✓ AutoFilter'.

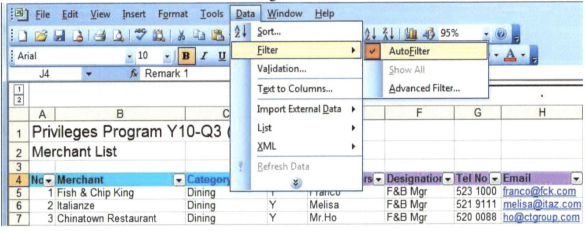

Tips 💡 **:**

1. Click 'Toolbar Options' at the right end next to the 'Font Color' > Select 'Add or Remove Buttons' > Click 'Customize'.

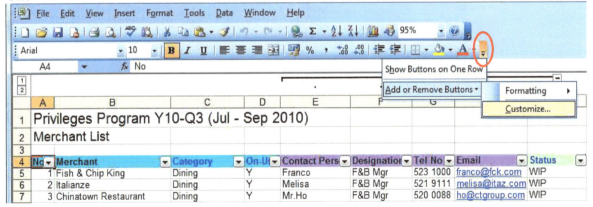

2. 'Customize' window appeared.
    In 'Commands' tab > Select Data > Click & Drag 'AutoFilter' to the toolbar.

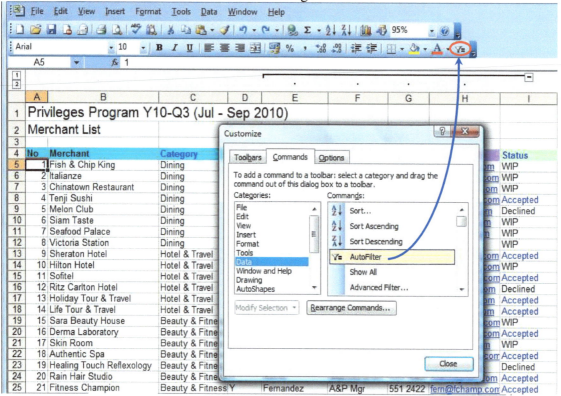

3. Back to 'Customize' window > Click & Drag 'Show All' this time to the end of toolbar.
    Close 'Customize' window.

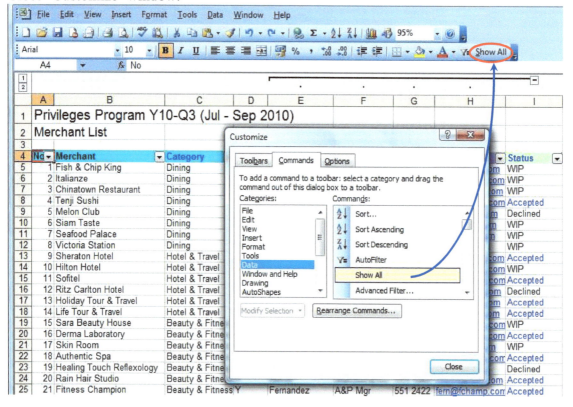

4. Place cell pointer at any cell within the header row, example at Cell A4 > Go to toolbar > Click 'AutoFilter' button.

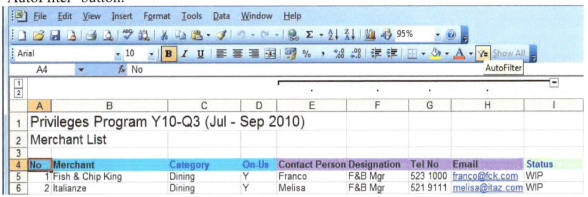

5. Performing filter on the selected field is the same with usual method.
   To show only merchants that still in WIP (Work-In-Progress), click at the 'Status' field drop-down list > Select 'WIP'.
   To further filter merchants under 'WIP' status that have 'Appointment Fixed' > Click at the 'Remark 1' field drop-down list > Select 'W – Appointment Fixed'.

6. To view all data again > Go to toolbar > Click 'Show All' button.

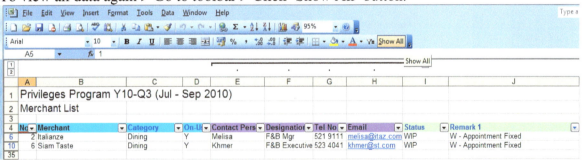

7. Removing 'Filter' is the same with usual method too.
   Click 'Data' menu again > 'Filter' > Deselect the ' ✓ AutoFilter'.

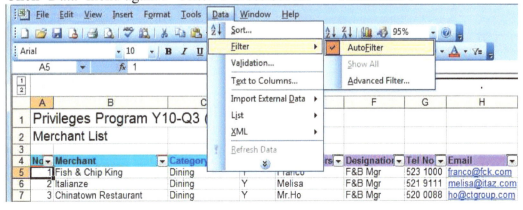

5.11 Sum only non-hidden row values, excludes hidden row values

Sometimes, there are list that you need to refer for just a few time OR in ad-hoc manner send by other people. In this situation, it is wasteful and inefficient to do a report to summarize the details in the list.

As such, apply 'Sum' within the list will be a faster way to get some information instantly. However, many facing a problem that the 'Sum' performed is for the whole list and cannot performed 'Sum' for the selected records/rows only.

Open workbook 'Tips 5.11.xls' to continue the tutorial.

Usual Method [using Hide Row]:
1. To find out the total purchase up-to-date in quantity using Hide Row > Place cell pointer at H26 > Click 'AutoSum' at toolbar.

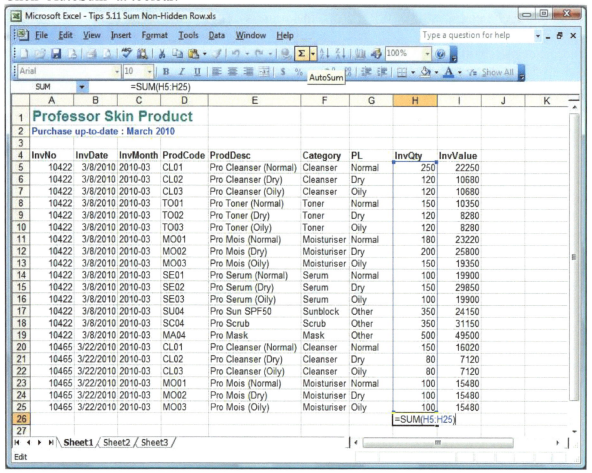

The total for the whole list is displayed at H26.

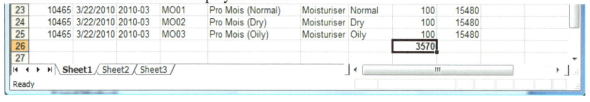

2. To view *Serum* product category only > Select row 5-13 & row 17-25 > Right Click on row heading > Click 'Hide'.

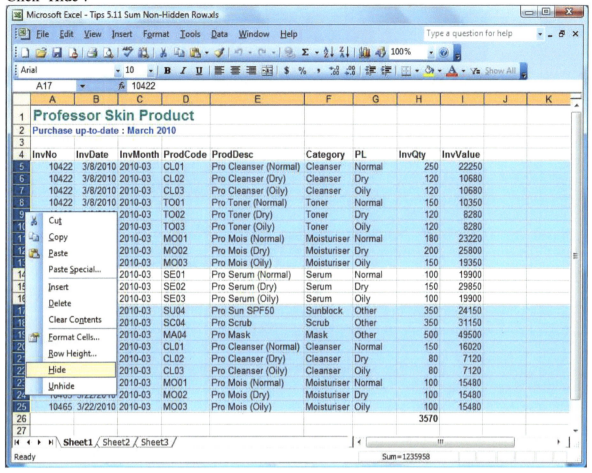

The list only shows *Serum* product records only but the total displayed is still total for the whole list instead of total for selected *Serum* product records only.

This is the problem that many users facing when using the list to sum instantly.

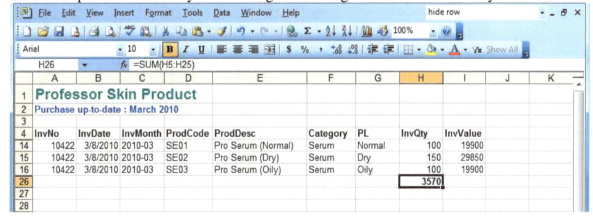

Usual Method [using AutoFilter]:

1. To find out the total purchase up-to-date in quantity using AutoFilter > Place cell pointer at A4 > Click 'AutoFilter' at toolbar.

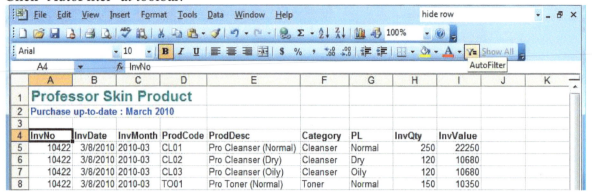

Place cell pointer at H28 > Click 'AutoSum' at toolbar.

Important: The sum has to be performed 2 rows away from the last record in order for the total to be displayed when filter is in used. If not, the total figure will be considered as part of the list and will be filtered out when you select the field's filtering criteria.

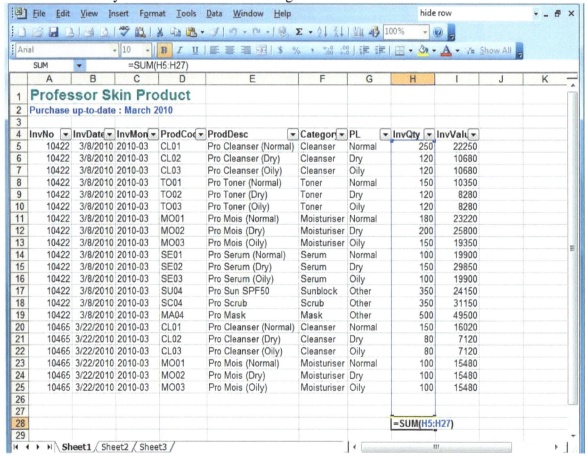

The total for the whole list is displayed at H28.

2. To view *Serum* product category only > Click at the 'Category' field drop-down list > Select 'Serum'.

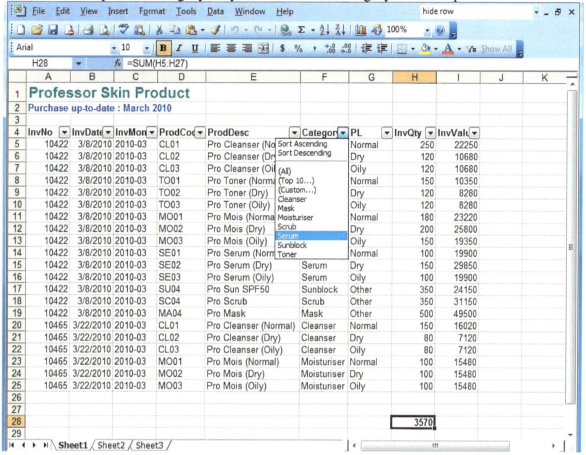

The list only shows *Serum* product records only but the total displayed is still total for the whole list instead of total for selected *Serum* product records only.

Same with 'AutoFilter' method, the users are still facing the same problem when using the list to sum instantly.

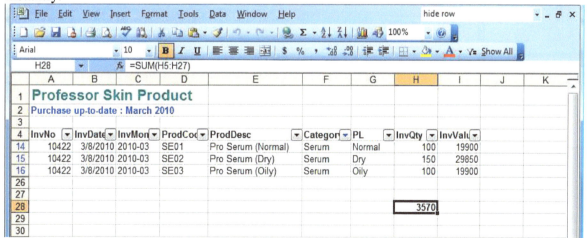

Tips ☝ [using Hide Row]:

1. Place cell pointer at H26 > Type '=SUBTOTAL(109, H5:H25)' > Press **ENTER** on keyboard.

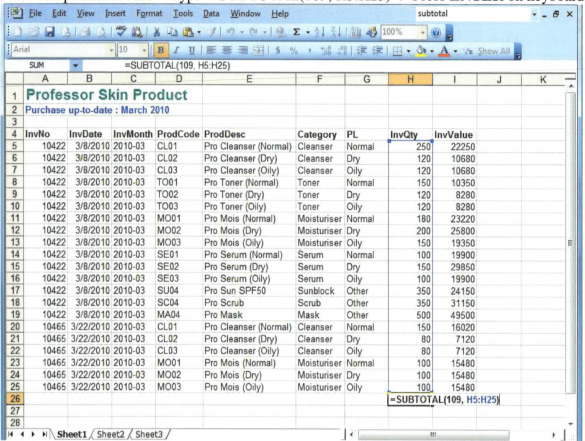

2. To view *Serum* product category only > Select row 5-13 & row 17-25 > Right Click on row heading > Click 'Hide'.

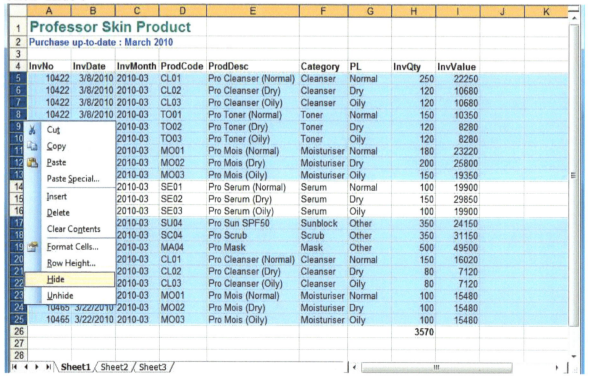

The list only shows *Serum* product records only and the total displayed is the total for selected *Serum* product records only. The subtotal function number '109' in the argument will only calculate the non-hidden row's value and ignores hidden row's value.

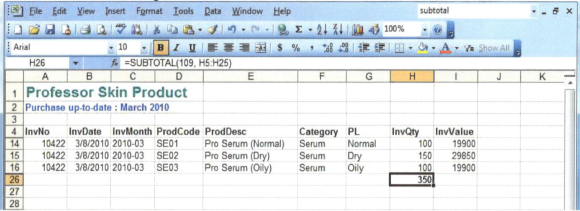

Tips ᵧ [using AutoFilter]:
1. Place cell pointer at A4 > Click 'AutoFilter' at toolbar.

Place cell pointer at H28 > Type '=SUBTOTAL(109, H5:H25)' > Press **ENTER** on keyboard.
Important: The sum has to be performed 2 rows away from the last record in order for the total to be displayed when filter is in used. If not, the total figure will be considered as part of the list and will be filtered out when you select the field's filtering criteria.

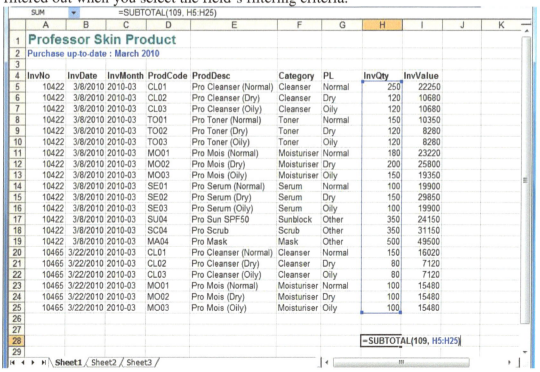

2. To view *Serum* product category only > > Click at the 'Category' field drop-down list > Select 'Serum'.

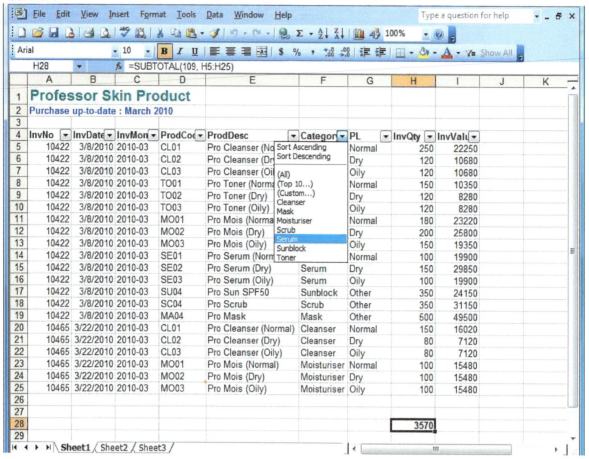

The list only shows *Serum* product records only and the total displayed is the total for selected *Serum* product records only. The subtotal function number '109' in the argument will only calculate the non-hidden row's value and ignores hidden row's value.

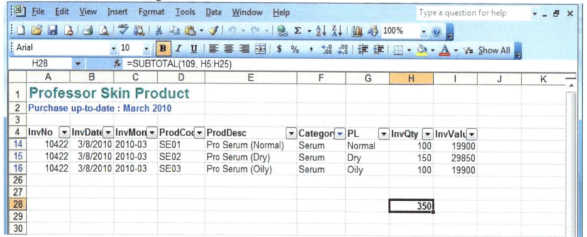

5.12 Update Cell [F9]

Workbook in idle situation do happened once in a while. The cells that contain formula do not update automatically even there is changes on it. In this situation, many people will close the file and re-open again.

Open workbook 'Tips 5.12.xls' to continue the tutorial.

Tips :
1. The formula in cell B2 returns current Date & Time of the system date.

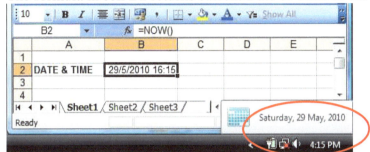

2. Minimize 'Tips 5.12.xls' workbook for few minutes.

3. The formula did not update automatically when it was idle for few minutes.

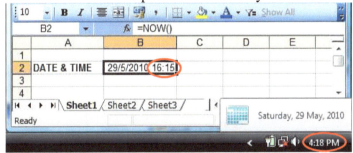

4. Place cell selector at B2 > Press 'F9' on keyboard.
    The cell has been updated without closing and re-opens the file.

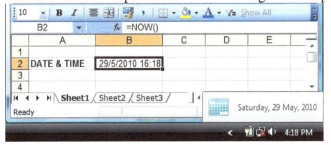

Thank you for purchasing ExcelAutomateReport©

Hope you have gained the skills, tips & concept of ExcelAutomateReport at the end of the chapter and start enjoy your journey now to automate reports in your work scenario.

Visit **www.eOfficeSolutionz.com** for updates OR

Email **careline@eofficesolutionz.com** for enquiry or feedback

ExcelAutomateReport©
Automatically prepare reports with just a few clicks !!!
By Ceyvian C